Anonymous

Royal Baker Pastry Cook

Anonymous

Royal Baker Pastry Cook

ISBN/EAN: 9783744788922

Printed in Europe, USA, Canada, Australia, Japan

Cover: Foto ©Lupo / pixelio.de

More available books at **www.hansebooks.com**

ROYAL· ·BAKER

Pastry ·Cook·

·By· ·Prof· G· Rudmani·

·Late· ·Chef· de· Cuisine· of· the· New· York· Cooking· School·

blished· by· the· ·Royal· Baking· Powder· ·Company·

106 Wall St· ·New·York·

A LETTER FROM MARION HARLAND.

[FAC SIMILE.]

I regard the Royal Baking Powder as the best manufactured and in the market, so far as I have any experience in the use of such compounds.

Since the introduction of it into my kitchen, three years ago, I have used no other in making biscuits, cake, etc., and have entirely discarded for such purposes the home made combination of one-third soda, two-thirds cream of tartar.

Every box has been in perfect condition when it came into my hands, and the contents have given complete satisfaction It is an act of simple justice and also a pleasure to recommend it unqualifiedly to American Housewives.

Brooklyn Marion Harland,
Nov 30, 1887.

GENERAL INDEX.

ALPHABETICAL INDEX TO RECEIPTS.

The cuts on this page represent pans used in the various kinds of baking, and are referred to in the Receipts according to numbers.

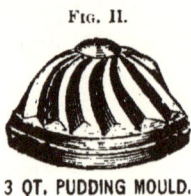

Fig. I.

2 QT. CAKE MOULD.

Fig. II.

3 QT. PUDDING MOULD.

Fig. III.

2 QT. CAKE MOULD.

Fig. IV.

3 QT. CAKE MOULD.

Fig. V.

TIMBALE MOULD.

Fig. VI.

PUDDING MOULD.

Fig. VII.

MUFFIN PANS.

Fig. VIII.

OVAL PUDDING PAN.

Fig. IX.

LEMON CAKE PAN.

Fig. X.

CAST GEM PANS.

Fig. XI.

WASH BRUSH.

Fig. XII.

TIN BREAD PAN.

Fig. XIII.

SQUARE CAKE PAN.

Fig. XIV.

BAKING SHEET.

Fig. XV.

ONE GALLON ICE CREAM FREEZER.

Fig. XVI.

FLOUR SIEVE.

Fig. XVII.

MUFFIN RINGS.

Fig. XVIII.

OVAL TIN PAN.

Fig. XIX.

WAFFLE IRON.

Fig. XX.

FAMILY SCALE.

DO NOT BUY BAKING POWDER LOOSE.—(What is meant by loose is weighing out in any quantity asked for.) All examinations made by Boards of Health, Government Chemists, and others, prove loose powders are, almost without exception, made from alum, and at a cost of about one-tenth of what a pure Cream Tartar powder, like the "ROYAL" Baking Powder, can be made for. The argument that the consumer will save in the purchase of such poisonous stuff, the cost of can, label, etc., is used simply to enable the seller to make a larger profit in selling an alum bulk, or loose powder at the expense of the unsuspecting consumer, than can be made by selling the absolutely pure "ROYAL" brand. Remember this, and insist on getting the "ROYAL" in cans.

Dr. Mott, the Government Chemist, in an article published in the *Scientific American*, exposes the deception carried on by selling loose or bulk poisonous baking powder. The label and trade-mark of some well-known and responsible manufacturer, the Doctor recommended as the best protection the public could have.

HINTS ON BAKING.

TO ACHIEVE PERFECT SUCCESS, the cook must use judgment and care. Some flour requires more water, or milk, than others; so that the quantity may have to be varied to make dough of a proper consistency. Different bakings will vary as to time and heat required, and should, therefore, be examined occasionally. To ascertain whether the bread is sufficiently done in center of the loaf or cake, thrust a clean straw or long thin splinter into it. If done there will be no dough on it when drawn out. Measure the flour, and be careful to mix with it the baking powder in a dry state, and before sifting. You can always substitute water for milk, or milk for water; butter for lard, or lard for butter. The number of eggs may be increased, diminished, or dispensed with entirely. Where fewer eggs are used than directed, always use a little more baking powder. Never use sour milk.

HEAT the bread knife very hot when about to cut new bread; this will prevent its crumbling.

CAKE BAKING.—For a plain cake made with one pound of flour, Royal Baking Powder, etc., the time to be allowed in baking would be from 40 to 50 minutes; at the outside not more than one hour. Very rich cakes, in which butter and eggs predominate, take, of course, very much longer time to bake, a pound cake taking from 1½ to 2 hours, and a bride's cake 3½. On no account should an oven be too hot when the cake is put in—that is, hot enough to brown at once; if so, in 5 minutes the whole outside will be burned and the interior will stand little chance of being baked. The old plan of feeling the handle of the oven door to test the heat is not always successful; it is better to sprinkle a little flour inside and shut the door for about 3 minutes; if at the end of that time it is of a rich light brown, the cake may be put in, but if burned the heat must be lessened.

In baking loaf cake, remember that unless you place a piece of paper over for protection at first, a top crust will be formed at once that prevents the raising. When cake is well raised remove paper for browning on top.

ADVICE TO THE COOK.—Great cleanliness, as well as care and attention, are required from a cook. Keep your hands *very* clean; try to prevent your nails from getting black and discolored; don't "scatter" in your kitchen, clean up as you go, put scalding water into each saucepan or stewpan as you finish using it. Dry your saucepans before you put them on the shelf. Never scrub inside of a fryingpan; rub it with wet silver-sand, rinse it out well with hot water afterwards. Wash your pudding-cloths, *scald* and hang them to dry directly after using them; air them before you put them away, or they will be musty; keep in dry place. Be careful not to use a knife that has cut onions till it has been cleaned. Keep sink and sink-brush very clean; be careful never to throw anything but water down sink. Do not throw cabbage water down it—throw it away out of doors, its smell is very bad. Never have sticky plates or dishes; use very hot water for washing them; when greasy, change it. Clean coppers with turpentine and fine brickdust, rubbed on with flannel, polish them with leather and a little dry brickdust. Clean your tins with soap and whiting mixed, made into a thick cream with hot water. Rub it on with flannel; when dry, whisk it off with clean leather and dry whiting. Take care that you look at the meat the butcher brings, to see that it is good. Let there be no waste in the kitchen.

Bread, Rolls and Muffins.

ROYAL UNFERMENTED BREAD.—1 quart flour, 1 teaspoonful salt, ½ teaspoonful sugar, 2 teaspoonfuls Royal Baking Powder, 1½ pints milk. Sift together thoroughly flour, salt, sugar, and powder; add the milk; mix smoothly and rapidly into a softer dough than can be handled. Turn from bowl into greased bread pan (fig. XII). Bake in moderate oven 45 minutes. Protect by placing paper on top during first fifteen minutes' baking.

German Unfermented Bread.—1 quart flour, 1½ tablespoonfuls sugar, 1 teaspoonful salt, 2 teaspoonfuls Royal Baking Powder, 1 large tablespoonful lard, 1 egg, 1 pint water. Sift together flour, sugar, salt, and powder, rub in the lard cold; add the beaten egg and water; mix into a smooth dough that can be handled. Flour the board, turn it out, form into shape of a loaf deftly as possible—don't handle much, but get it into a greased tin (fig. XII). Bake in fair, steady oven for 45 minutes. Protect the loaf with paper 20 minutes.

Graham Unfermented Bread.—1½ pints Graham flour, ½ pint flour, 1 tablespoonful sugar, 1 teaspoonful salt, two teaspoonfuls Royal Baking Powder, 1¼ pints milk, or equal parts milk and water. Sift together Graham flour, flour, sugar, salt, and powder; add the milk, or milk and water; mix rapidly into soft dough, which pour from bowl into greased tin (fig. XII). Bake in rather hot oven 40 minutes. Protect loaf with paper first 15 minutes.

Boston Brown Bread.—Flour ½ pint, 1 pint corn meal, ½ pint rye flour, 2 potatoes, 1 teaspoonful salt, 1 tablespoonful brown sugar, 2 teaspoonfuls Royal Baking Powder, ½ pint water. Sift flour, corn meal, rye flour, sugar, salt and powder together thoroughly; peel, wash and boil well 2 mealy potatoes, rub them through sieve, diluting with water. When this is quite cold use it to mix flour, etc., into batter like cake; pour into well greased mold (fig. VI), having a cover. Place it in saucepan half full of boiling water, where the loaf will simmer 1 hour, without water getting into it. Remove it then, take off cover, finish by baking in fairly hot oven 30 minutes.

Norwegian Bread (For Dyspeptics).—1 pint barley meal, ½ pint Graham flour, ½ pint flour, 1 teaspoonful salt, two teaspoonfuls Royal Baking Powder, 1 pint milk. Sift together barley meal, Graham flour, flour, salt, and powder; mix into firm batter with the milk; pour into greased tin (fig. XII), bake in moderate oven 40 minutes. Cover with paper 25 minutes.

Oatmeal Bread.—½ pint oatmeal, 1½ of flour, ½ teaspoonful salt, 3 of Royal Baking Powder, ¾ pint milk. Boil oatmeal in 1½ pints salted water one hour; add milk; set aside until cold. Then place in bowl, sift together flour, salt, and powder, and add. Mix smoothly and deftly. Bake in greased tin (fig. XII) 45 minutes, protected with paper 20 minutes.

Peculiars.—1 pint flour sifted with 1 teaspoonful Royal Baking Powder, a little salt, one egg; mix with one pint sweet milk, beat well to a batter, and bake quick in buttered "Gem" pans already hot.

THE ROYAL BAKING POWDER IS ABSOLUTELY PURE.

Brown Bread. — Corn meal 1 pint, 1 pint rye flour, 1 teaspoonful brown sugar, 1 teaspoonful salt, 2 teaspoonfuls Royal Baking Pow er, 1 tablespoonful lard, ¾ pint milk. Sift together corn meal, rye flour, sugar, salt and powder. Rub in the lard cold; add the milk, and mix the whole into a batter like cake. Pour into greased tin (fig. XII), and bake 40 minutes in rather hot oven. Protect at first with paper.

Graham Lunch Bread. — 1½ pints Graham flour, ½ pint flour, 1 tablespoonful sugar, 1 teaspoonful salt, 2 teaspoonfuls Royal Baking Powder, ¾ pint of milk. Sift together Graham flour, flour, sugar, salt and powder, add the milk; mix into smooth dough that can be easily handled. Flour the board, turn out dough, give it a quick, vigorous additional kneading to complete its smoothness; then divide into four large pieces, which form into long loaves, lay them just touching in a square shallow cake pan (fig. XIII), wash them over with milk. Bake in rather hot oven 30 minutes. When removing from oven rub them over with a little butter on a clean piece of linen.

Corn Bread (New Orleans). — 1½ pints corn meal, ½ pint flour, 1 tablespoonful sugar, 1 teaspoonful salt, two heaping teaspoonfuls Royal Baking Powder, 1 tablespoonful lard, 1¼ pints milk, 2 eggs. Sift together corn meal, flour, sugar, salt, and powder; rub in lard cold, add eggs (beaten), and the milk; mix into a moderately stiff batter; pour from bowl into shallow cake pan (fig. XIII). Bake in rather hot oven 30 minutes.

Delicate Graham Bread (for Invalids). — 1 pint Graham flour, 1 pint flour, 1 teaspoonful sugar, 1 of salt, 2 of Royal Baking Powder. Sift all well together, rejecting coarse bran left in sieve. Add 1½ pints milk. Mix quickly into smooth, soft dough. Bake in 2 small greased tins (fig. XII) 25 minutes. Protect with paper 10 minutes.

Rye Bread. — 1 pint rye flour, ½ pint corn meal, ½ pint flour, 1 teaspoonful sugar, 1 teaspoonful salt, 2 teaspoonfuls Royal Baking Powder, 1 tablespoonful lard, ¾ pint milk. Sift together rye flour, corn meal, flour, sugar, salt, and powder; rub in lard cold; add milk; mix into smooth batter, as for cake; pour into well-greased tin (fig. XII), bake in moderate oven 45 minutes. Protect loaf with paper first 20 minutes.

Graham Rolls. — 1 pint Graham flour, 1 pint flour, 1 teaspoonful salt, 2 teaspoonfuls Royal Baking Powder, 1 tablespoonful lard, ¾ pint milk. Sift together Graham flour, flour, salt, and powder; rub in lard cold; add milk, and mix the whole into smooth dough that can be handled — not *too* soft; flour board, turn it out, and form into rolls shape and size of large fingers. Lay them on baking sheet (fig. XIV), so they will not touch. Wash their surfaces with soft brush (fig. XI), dipped in milk to glaze them. Bake in hot oven from 10 to 12 minutes.

Lunch Rolls. — 1 quart flour, 1 teaspoonful salt, 2 teaspoonfuls Royal Baking Powder, 1 tablespoonful lard, 1 pint milk. Sift together flour, salt, and powder; rub in lard cold; add milk, mix to a smooth dough to be easily handled. Flour the board, turn out dough, give 1 or 2 quick kneadings to give it smoothness. Roll out little over ⅓ inch thick, cut out with round cutter about 2½ inches in diameter; lay them on greased baking tin (fig. XIV), just touching (in rows evenly), wash over with milk, bake in fairly hot oven 25 minutes. Wash them over again with milk when taken from oven.

French Muffins. — 1½ pints flour, 1 cupful honey, ½ teaspoonful salt, 2 teaspoonfuls Royal Baking Powder, 2 tablespoonfuls butter, 3 eggs, and little over ½ pint milk or thin cream. Sift together flour, salt, and powder; rub in butter, cold; add beaten eggs, milk, or thin cream, and honey. Mix smoothly into batter as for pound cake; about ½ fill sponge cake tins, cold and carefully greased, and bake in good, steady oven 7 or 8 minutes.

Breakfast Rolls. — 1½ pints flour, ½ pint corn meal (white), 1 teaspoonful salt, 2 teaspoonfuls Royal Baking Powder, 1 tablespoonful lard, ¾ pint milk. Sift together flour, corn meal, salt, and powder; rub in lard cold, add the milk, mix smoothly into rather firmer dough than usual. Flour the board, turn out the dough, give it 1 or 2 turns to complete its smoothness, Divide it, thus prepared, into pieces size of an egg; again divide these in half, which roll out under the hand until they are long and half the size of one's little finger. Lay on greased baking tin (fig. XIV), so that they do not touch, wash them over with milk, bake in hot oven 7 or 8 minutes.

Dinner Rolls. — 1 quart flour, 1 teaspoonful sugar, 1 teaspoonful salt, 2 teaspoonfuls Royal Baking Powder, 2 tablespoonfuls lard, ¾ pint milk. Sift together flour, sugar, salt, and powder; rub in the lard cold, add the milk, and mix into smooth, rather stiffer dough than usual. Flour the board, turn out the dough, give it 1 or 2 quick, vigorous kneadings to complete its smoothness. Roll out about ⅓ of it at a time with rolling-pin, very thin, cut in three-inch strips, then roll these strips up tight; they should be the thickness of a large lead pencil, as long as can be conveniently laid on greased baking tin (fig. XIV). (The longer the rolls are when baked, the nicer they are). Bake in a pretty hot oven 8 or 10 minutes. They need to be crisp and not too dark colored.

Vienna Twist Rolls. — Divide the dough, as described for Vienna rolls, size of a small egg, then divide each piece in 2 unequal pieces, largest piece form with hands into plain roll tapering at each end; lay them thus formed on greased baking tin (fig. XIV), without touching, flatten each a little and wash over with milk, divide remaining pieces each into 3, roll pieces out under the hands into strips a little longer than roll already made, and braid them; then lay each braid soon as formed on top of other plain half; when all are made wash over with milk. Bake in hot oven 20 minutes. A very handsome roll for dinner party. ·

Boston Muffins. — 1½ pints flour, ½ pint corn meal, 1 tablespoonful sugar, 1 teaspoonful salt, 2 teaspoonfuls Royal Baking Powder, 1 tablespoonful butter, 3 eggs, and one pint (full measure) milk, 1 teaspoonful Royal Extract Cinnamon. Sift together flour, corn meal, sugar, salt, and powder; rub in lard cold, add eggs, beaten, milk, and extract cinnamon; mix into batter a little stiffer than ordinary griddle cake batter; have griddle heated regularly all over, grease it, lay on it muffin rings, also greased; half fill them with batter. As soon as risen to tops of rings, turn them over gently with cake turner; bake nice brown on either side. They should bake in 7 or 8 minutes.

Rice Muffins. — 2 cupfuls cold boiled rice, 1 pint flour, 1 teaspoonful salt, 1 tablespoonful sugar, 1½ teaspoonfuls Royal Baking Powder, ½ pint milk, 3 eggs. Dilute rice, free from lumps, with milk and beaten eggs; sift together flour, sugar, salt, and powder; add to rice preparation, mix into smooth, rather firm batter; muffin pans (fig. VII) to be cold and well greased, then fill ⅔; bake in hot oven 15 minutes.

Royal Sally Lunn Muffins. — 1 quart flour, 1 tablespoonful sugar, 1 teaspoonful salt, 3 teaspoonfuls Royal Baking Powder, 1 tablespoonful lard, 1 egg, 1¼ pints milk. Sift together flour, sugar, salt and powder; rub in lard cold; add egg, beaten, and milk; mix into rather firm batter; muffin pans to be cold and well greased, then fill ⅔. Bake in hot oven 15 minutes.

Rye Muffins. — 1 pint rye flour, ½ pint corn meal, ½ pint flour, 1 teaspoonful sugar, 1 teaspoonful salt, 3 teaspoonfuls Royal Baking Powder, 1 tablespoonful lard, 2 eggs, 1 pint milk. Sift together rye flour, corn meal, flour, sugar, salt, and powder; rub in lard cold; add beaten eggs, and milk; mix into smooth, rather firm batter; muffin pans to be cold and well greased, then fill ⅔. Bake in hot oven 15 minutes.

THE ROYAL BAKING POWDER IS ABSOLUTELY PURE.

French Rolls.—1 quart flour, 1 teaspoonful salt, 2 teaspoonfuls Royal Baking Powder, 1 tablespoonful lard, nearly 1 pint milk. Sift flour, salt, and lard together thoroughly; rub in lard cold, add milk, and mix into rather firmer dough than ordinary Flour board, turn out dough, and immediately give it 1 or 2 quick, vigorous kneadings to complete its smoothness. Now divide it into pieces size of egg, then each piece in half, which form under the hands into appearance of short thick rolls tapering sharply at each end. Put two of these pieces together side by side, pinching ends together a little, lay them on greased baking tin (fig. XIV), wash over with milk. Bake in hot oven 15 minutes.

Royal Corn Muffins.—1 pint corn meal, 1 pint flour, 1 tablespoonful sugar, 1 teaspoonful salt, 3 teaspoonfuls Royal Baking Powder, 1 tablespoonful lard, 2 eggs, 1 pint milk. Sift together corn meal, flour, sugar, salt, and powder; rub in lard cold, and eggs beaten, and milk; mix into batter of consistence of cup cake; muffin pans to be cold and well greased, then fill ⅔. Bake in hot oven fifteen minutes.

Vienna Rolls.—1 quart flour, ½ teaspoonful salt, 2 teaspoonfuls Royal Baking Powder, 1 tablespoonful lard, 1 pint milk. Sift together flour, salt, and powder; rub in lard cold, add milk, and mix *in the bowl* into smooth dough, easily handled without sticking to hands and board. Flour board, turn out dough and give it a quick knead or two to equalize it; then roll it out with rolling-pin to thickness of ½ inch, cut out with large round cutter, fold ½ over the other by doubling it; lay them on greased baking sheet (fig. XIV), without touching. Wash them over with a little milk to glaze them. Bake in hot oven 15 minutes.

English Muffins.—1 quart flour, ½ teaspoonful sugar, 1 teaspoonful salt, 2 large teaspoonfuls Royal Baking Powder, 1¼ pints milk. Sift together flour, sugar, salt, and powder; add milk, and mix into smooth batter trifle stiffer than for griddle cakes. Have griddle heated regularly all over, grease it and lay on muffin rings (fig. XVII), half fill them and when risen well up to top of rings turn over gently with cake turner. They should not be too brown, just a buff color. When all cooked, pull each open in half, toast delicately, butter well, serve on folded napkin, piled high and very hot.

Graham Muffins.—1 quart Graham flour, 1 tablespoonful brown sugar, 1 teaspoonful salt, 3 teaspoonfuls Royal Baking Powder, 1 egg, 1 pint milk. Sift together Graham flour, sugar, salt, and powder, add beaten egg and milk; mix into batter like pound cake, muffin pans (fig. VII), well greased, ⅔ full; bake in hot oven 15 minutes.

Oatmeal Muffins.—1 cup of oatmeal, 1½ pints flour, 1 teaspoonful salt, 2 teaspoonfuls Royal Baking Powder, 1 tablespoonful lard, 2 eggs, 1 pint milk. Sift together oatmeal, flour, salt, and powder; rub in lard cold, add beaten eggs and milk; mix smoothly into batter rather thinner than cup cake; fill muffin pans (fig. VII) ⅔ full; bake in good hot oven 15 minutes.

"Poor Man's" Corn Gems.—1 pint corn meal, 1 pint flour, 1 teaspoonful salt, 2 teaspoonfuls Royal Baking Powder, ½ pint each of milk and water. Sift the corn meal, flour, salt, and powder together. Add the milk and water, mix into a firm batter; ⅔ fill well greased, cold gem pans (fig. X). Bake in a well heated oven 15 minutes.

Royal Egg Muffins.—1 quart flour, 1 tablespoonful sugar, 1 tablespoonful salt, 1 large tablespoonful lard, 2 teaspoonfuls Royal Baking Powder, 3 eggs, 1¼ pints milk. Sift together flour, sugar, salt, and powder; rub in the lard cold; add the beaten eggs and milk; mix quickly into a smooth batter, a little firmer than for griddle cakes; ⅔ fill cold, carefully greased muffin pans (fig. VII); bake in hot oven 15 minutes.

Royal Graham Gems.—1½ pints Graham, ½ pint corn meal, 1 teaspoonful salt, 2 teaspoonfuls Royal Baking Powder, 1¼ pints milk. Sift together Graham, corn meal, salt, and powder. Add the milk, and mix into a moderately stiff batter. ½ fill cold gem pans (fig. X), well greased. Bake in a solid hot oven 10 to 12 minutes.

Biscuit, Buns, Etc.

BREAKFAST BISCUIT.—Take 1 quart sweet milk, ½ cupful melted butter, a little salt, 2 tablespoonfuls Royal Baking Powder, flour enough to make a stiff batter; do not knead into dough, but drop into buttered tins from a spoon; bake in a hot oven—unless it is hot they will not be light and tender.

Hot Biscuit.—1 quart flour, 1 teaspoonful salt, 3 teaspoonfuls Royal Baking Powder, 1 tablespoonful lard, 1 pint sweet milk, cold (never use sour milk); use cold water when milk cannot be obtained. Sift together flour, salt, and powder; rub in lard cold; add milk, form into smooth, consistent dough. Flour the board, turn out dough, roll out to thickness of ¾ inch, cut with small round cutter; lay them close together on greased baking tin; bake in good hot oven. Old biscuit can be made fresh by moistening, placing in oven until heated through.

English Biscuits.—1½ pints flour, 1 coffeecupful corn starch, 3 tablespoonfuls sugar, large pinch salt, 2 teaspoonfuls Royal Baking Powder, 3 tablespoonfuls lard, 1 egg, ½ pint milk, ½ cup currants, 1 tablespoonful coriander seed (if desired). Sift together flour, corn starch, sugar, salt, and powder; rub in lard cold; add eggs, beaten, milk, currants (well washed), picked, and dried, and coriander seeds; mix into smooth dough, soft enough to handle. Flour the board, turn out dough, roll to ½ inch thickness, cut with round cutter, lay them on greased baking tin (fig. XIV), bake in rather hot oven 20 minutes. Rub over with little butter on clean piece of linen, when taken from oven.

Lemon Biscuit.—1 cupful butter, 2½ cupfuls sugar, 4 eggs, 1½ pints flour, 1 teaspoonful Royal Baking Powder, 1 teaspoonful Royal Extract *Lemon*. Mix the butter, sugar, and beaten eggs, smooth; add the flour, sifted with the powder, and the extract. Flour the board, roll out the dough ¼ inch thick, and cut out with a large round cutter, lay out on a greased tin (fig. XIV), wash over with milk, and lay a thin slice of citron on each. Bake in hot oven 10 minutes.

London Crumpets.—1½ pints flour, ½ teaspoonful salt, 1 teaspoonful sugar, 2 teaspoonfuls Royal Baking Powder, 1 egg, nearly a pint milk and cream in equal parts, 1 teaspoonful Royal Extract *Cinnamon*. Sift together flour, salt, sugar and powder; add beaten egg, milk, cream and extract; mix into rather firm batter, half fill large greased muffin rings (fig. XVII) on hot, well greased griddle; bake on one side of them only. Serve hot with cottage cheese.

Sugar Biscuit.—1½ pints flour, pinch salt, 1 coffeecupful sugar, 2 teaspoonfuls Royal Baking Powder, 1 tablespoonful lard, 2 eggs, ½ pint milk, 1 teaspoonful Royal Extract *Nutmeg*. Sift together flour, salt, sugar and powder; rub in lard cold; add beaten eggs and milk; mix in smooth batter as for muffins, drop with tablespoon on greased baking tin (fig. XIV); sift sugar over tops; bake in hot oven 8 or 10 minutes.

Sweet Potato Buns.—3 large sweet potatoes, 1½ pints flour, pinch salt, 1½ teaspoonfuls Royal Baking Powder, 1 pint cream. Boil potatoes tender, rub them very fine with cream. Sift together flour, salt and powder; add to potato preparation; mix into rather firm, smooth dough; form into round pieces size of small egg; lay on greased tin (fig. XIV); bake in hot oven 20 minutes.

Abernethy Biscuit. —3 pints flour, 2 tablespoonfuls sugar, 1 teaspoonful salt, 1½ teaspoonfuls Royal Baking Powder, 4 tablespoonfuls lard, 2 tablespoonfuls caraway seeds, 2 eggs, 1 pint milk. Sift together flour, sugar, salt and powder, rub in lard cold, add seeds, beaten eggs, and milk; mix into smooth, firm dough. Flour the board, turn out the dough, give it a few quick vigorous kneadings, roll out to thickness of ¼ inch. Cut into biscuits the size of pudding saucer, prick with fork, lay on greased baking tin fig. XIV), bake in rather hot oven 15 minutes. Store when cold.

Waffles, Puffs, Etc.

GERMAN WAFFLES. —1 quart flour, ½ teaspoonful salt, 3 tablespoonfuls sugar, 2 large teaspoonfuls Royal Baking Powder, 2 tablespoonfuls lard, rind of 1 lemon, grated, 1 teaspoonful Royal Extract *Cinnamon,* 4 eggs, and 1 pint thin cream. Sift together flour, sugar, salt, and powder; rub in lard cold; add beaten eggs, lemon rind, extract and milk. Mix into smooth, rather thick batter. Bake in hot waffle-iron, serve with sugar flavored with Royal Extract of *Lemon.*

Soft Waffles. —1 quart flour, ½ teaspoonful salt, 1 teaspoonful sugar, 2 teaspoonfuls Royal Baking Powder, 1 large tablespoonful butter, 2 eggs, 1½ pints milk. Sift together flour, salt, sugar and powder; rub in butter cold; add beaten eggs and milk; mix into smooth consistent batter, that will run easily and limpid from mouth of pitcher. Have waffle-iron hot, and carefully greased each time; fill ⅔, close it up, when brown turn over. Sift sugar on them, serve hot.

German Puffs. —1 pint flour, 2 tablespoonfuls sugar, pinch of salt, 1½ teaspoonfuls Royal Baking Powder, 3 tablespoonfuls butter, 4 eggs, 2 ounces sweet almonds, 3 drops Royal Extract *Bitter Almonds,* ½ pint cream, ½ cupful sultana raisins, ½ wineglass rum. Rub butter and sugar to white, light cream; add eggs (whole) 1 at a time, beating three or four minutes between each addition; blanch the almonds. (See receipt for Almond Pudding.) Sift together flour, salt and powder, which add to butter, etc., with almonds, raisins, extract bitter almonds, cream and rum. Mix whole together into smooth batter as for pound cake; ⅔ fill well greased cups; bake in fairly hot oven 20 minutes; at end of that time insert straw gently. If it comes out clean they are ready; if any of uncooked batter adheres to straw, must be set carefully back few minutes longer.

Golden Johnny Cake. —Cook in steamer and pulp fine 1 fine grain squash (Hubbard is best), thicken 1 pint sweet milk with the squash pulp until the consistency of rich cream, sweeten lightly with white sugar. Take 3 parts Indian meal, 1 part best flour, the quantity being sufficient to make usual Johnny cake batter. Add about two teaspoonfuls Royal Baking Powder, ½ teacupful raisins, 1 teacupful currants, 1 pinch salt. A little good butter worked in when pulping the squash improves the cake.

Graham Flour Puffs. —1½ pints Graham flour, 1 teaspoonful salt, 2 large teaspoonfuls Royal Baking Powder, 2 eggs and 1 pint milk. Sift together Graham, salt and powder, add beaten eggs and milk; mix together into smooth batter, as for cup cake, half fill cold gem pans (fig. X), well greased, bake in hot oven 10 minutes.

Johnny Cake (New England). —1 pint corn meal, 1 pint flour, ½ cupful sugar, ½ teaspoonful salt, 1 tablespoonful lard, 2 teaspoonfuls Royal Baking Powder, 3 eggs, and 1¼ pints milk. Sift together corn meal, flour, sugar, salt and powder; rub in lard cold; add beaten eggs and milk; mix into firm, smooth batter, pour into square shallow cake pan (fig. XIII). Bake in rather hot oven 45 minutes.

Royal Sally Lunns. —1 quart flour, 1 teaspoonful salt, 2 teaspoonfuls Royal Baking Powder, ⅔ cup butter, 4 eggs, ½ pint milk. Sift together flour, salt, and powder; rub in butter cold; add beaten eggs and milk; mix into firm batter like cup cake, pour into two round cake tins size of pie plates; bake 25 minutes in pretty hot oven, or until a straw thrust into them gently comes up free of dough.

Rusks. —1½ pints flour, ½ teaspoonful salt, 2 tablespoonfuls sugar, 2 teaspoonfuls Royal Baking Powder, 2 tablespoonfuls lard, 3 eggs, 1 teaspoonful each Royal Extract *Nutmeg* and *Cinnamon,* ¾ pint milk. Sift together flour, salt, sugar and powder; rub in lard cold; add milk, beaten eggs and extracts. Mix into dough soft enough to handle; flour the board, turn out dough, give it quick turn or two to complete its smoothness. Roll them under the hands into round balls size of a small egg; lay them on greased shallow cake pan (fig. XIII), put very close together; bake in moderately heated oven 30 minutes; when cold sift sugar over them.

Rice Waffles. —Into a batter as directed for *Soft Waffles,* stir 1 cupful of rice, free from lumps; cook as directed in same receipt.

Scotch Short Bread. —1½ pints flour, ½ teaspoonful salt, 4 tablespoonfuls sugar, 4 tablespoonfuls butter, 1 teaspoonful Royal Baking Powder, 3 eggs, 1 teacupful milk, 1 teaspoonful Royal Extract of *Orange.* Sift together flour, sugar, salt and powder; rub in butter cold; add beaten eggs, nearly all the milk and extract, mix into smooth dough without much handling. Flour the board, turn out dough, roll with the rolling-pin to ¼ inch in thickness, cut with knife into shape of small envelopes, lay them on a baking tin (fig. XIV), wash them over with remainder of milk, lay on each three large, thin slices citron and few caraway seeds. Bake in moderate hot oven 20 minutes.

Crackers.

CORN STARCH CRACKERS. —1½ pints flour, ½ pint corn starch, ½ teaspoonful salt, 1 tablespoonful sugar, 1 tablespoonful lard, 1 teaspoonful Royal Baking Powder, ½ pint milk. Sift together flour, corn starch, salt, sugar and powder; rub in lard cold; add milk, and mix into smooth, firm dough. Flour the board a little, turn out dough, give few quick, vigorous kneadings to complete smoothness. Set it under cloth 10 minutes. Then roll it with rolling-pin exceedingly thin, cut with round cutter, prick each cracker with fork, lay upon slightly greased baking tin (fig. XIV), wash over with milk, bake in hot oven 7 or 8 minutes. When cold, store them for use.

Graham Crackers. —1 quart best Graham flour, 1 tablespoonful sugar, ½ teaspoonful salt, ½ teaspoonful Royal Baking Powder, 2 tablespoonfuls butter, little more than ½ pint milk. Sift together Graham, sugar, salt, and powder; rub in lard cold, add milk, mix into smooth, consistent dough. Flour the board, turn out dough, knead well 5 minutes. Roll with rolling-pin to thickness of ¼ inch; cut with knife into small envelope-shaped crackers. Bake in rather hot oven with care (as they burn readily) 10 minutes. Handle carefully while hot; when cold store for use.

Gem Crackers. —1½ pints flour, ½ pint corn meal, 1 teaspoonful salt, 1 teaspoonful Royal Baking Powder, 2 tablespoonfuls butter, little more than ⅔ pint milk. Sift together flour, corn meal, salt, powder; rub in butter cold; add milk, mix into smooth, rather firm dough. Flour the board, turn out dough, give it a turn or two quickly, roll to thickness of ¼ inch. Cut with small oval cutter, prick each cracker with a fork, lay them on greased baking tin (fig. XIV), wash over with milk, and bake in hot oven 8 to 10 minutes.

Egg Cracknels (Cream Crackers).—1 quart flour, large pinch salt, 5 tablespoonfuls sugar, 1 teaspoonful Royal Baking Powder, 4 tablespoonfuls butter, 5 eggs. Sift together flour, sugar, salt, and powder; rub in butter cold, add eggs, beaten, and mix into firm, smooth dough. Flour board, turn out dough, give it few minutes rapid kneading; cover with damp towel 15 minutes, then roll out to thickness of ¼ inch. Cut with biscuit cutter. When all cut, have large pot boiling, and large tin pan cold water. Drop them, few at a time, into the boiling water. When they appear at surface, and curl at edges, take them up with skimmer, and drop them into the cold water. When all are thus served, lay on greased baking tins and bake in fairly hot oven 15 minutes.

Rice Flour Crackers.—Proceed as directed for Corn Starch Crackers; substitute rice flour for starch.

Griddle Cakes, Etc.

GRAHAM GRIDDLE CAKES.—1 pint Graham flour, ½ pint corn meal, ½ pint flour, 1 heaping teaspoonful brown sugar, ½ teaspoonful salt, 2 teaspoonfuls Royal Baking Powder, 1 egg, ½ pint each of milk and water. Sift together Graham flour, corn meal, flour, sugar, salt, and powder. Add beaten egg, milk and water. Mix together into a smooth batter without being too thin (if too thick it will not run but break off and drop.) Heat griddle *hot*, pour batter into cakes as large as a tea saucer. Bake brown on one side, carefully turn and brown other side. Pile one on the other, serve very hot, with sugar, milk, cream, or maple syrup.

Geneva Griddle Cakes.—1½ pints flour, 4 tablespoonfuls sugar, ½ teaspoonful salt, 1½ teaspoonfuls Royal Baking Powder, 2 tablespoonfuls butter, 4 eggs, nearly ½ pint milk. Rub to white, light cream butter and sugar, add yelks of eggs, 1 at a time. Sift flour, salt, and powder together; add to butter, etc., with milk and egg whites whipped to dry froth; mix together into a smooth batter. Bake in small cakes; as soon as brown turn, and brown the other side. Have buttered baking tin; fast as browned, lay them on it, and spread raspberry jam over them; then bake more, which lay on others already done. Repeat this until you have used jam twice, then bake another batch, which use to cover them. Sift sugar plentifully over them, place in a moderate oven to finish cooking.

Huckleberry Griddle Cakes.—½ pint huckleberries, 1½ pints flour, 1 teaspoonful salt, 1 tablespoonful brown sugar, 2 teaspoonfuls Royal Baking Power, 2 eggs, 1 pint milk. Sift together flour, sugar, salt, and powder; add beaten eggs, milk, and huckleberries (washed and picked over). Mix into batter that will run from pitcher in thick, continuous stream. Have griddle hot enough to form crust soon as batter touches it. In order to confine juice of berries, turn quickly, so as to form crust on other side; turn once more on each side to complete baking. Blackberry or Raspberry Griddle Cakes in same manner.

Rye Griddle Cakes.—1 pint rye flour, ½ pint Graham flour, ½ pint flour, 1 tablespoonful sugar, ½ teaspoonful salt, 2 teaspoonfuls Royal Baking Powder, 1 egg and 1 pint milk. Sift together rye flour, Graham flour, sugar, salt, and baking powder, add beaten egg and milk, mix into smooth batter. Bake deep brown color on hot griddle.

Rice Griddle Cakes.—2 cupfuls cold boiled rice, 1 pint flour, 1 teaspoonful sugar, ½ teaspoonful salt, 1½ teaspoonfuls Royal Baking Powder, 1 egg, little more than ½ pint milk. Sift together flour, sugar, salt and powder; add rice free from lumps, diluted with beaten egg and milk; mix into smooth batter. Have griddle well heated, make cakes large, bake nicely brown, serve with maple syrup.

Crushed Wheat Griddle Cakes.—1 cupful crushed wheat, 1½ pints flour, 1 teaspoonful brown sugar, ½ teaspoonful salt, 2 teaspoonfuls Royal Baking Powder, 1 egg, 1 pint milk. Boil 1 cupful crushed wheat in ¾ pint of water 1 hour, then dilute with beaten egg and milk. Sift together flour, sugar, salt, and powder; add to crushed wheat preparation when quite cold, mix into smooth batter. Bake on hot griddle; brown delicately on both sides; serve with Hygienic Cream Sauce.

Indian Griddle Cakes.—⅔ quart corn meal, ⅓ quart flour, 1 teaspoonful brown sugar, ½ teaspoonful salt, 2 heaping teaspoonfuls Royal Baking Powder, 2 eggs, 1 pint milk. Sift together corn meal, flour, salt, sugar, and powder, add beaten eggs and milk, mix into a smooth batter. Bake on very hot griddle to a nice brown. Serve with molasses or maple syrup.

Bread Griddle Cakes.—½ lb. bread, 1 pint flour, 1 teaspoonful brown sugar, ½ teaspoonful salt, 1½ teaspoonfuls Royal Baking Powder, ¾ pint milk, 1 egg. Put bread, free from crust, to steep in warm water. When thoroughly soaked, wring dry in a towel; dilute with beaten egg and milk. Sift together flour, sugar, salt, and powder; add to prepared bread, mix together into a smooth batter. Bake on well heated griddle. Serve with sugar and cream.

Quick Buckwheat Cakes No. 1.—To 1 pint buckwheat flour, while dry, add 2 heaping teaspoonfuls Royal Baking Powder, teaspoonful salt, 1 scant tablespoonful brown sugar or New Orleans molasses to make them brown, mix well together; when ready to bake add 1 pint cold water or sufficient to form a batter, stir but little, bake immediately on hot griddle. The baking powder should never be put into batter, but always mixed with flour in dry state. Some prefer addition of a little wheat flour and Indian meal, like No. 2.

Buckwheat Cakes No. 2.—To 1½ pints pure buckwheat flour, add ¼ pint each wheat flour and Indian meal, 3 heaping teaspoonfuls Royal Baking Powder, 1 teaspoonful salt, 1 tablespoonful brown sugar or molasses. Sift well together in dry state, buckwheat, Indian meal, wheat flour, and baking powder, then add remainder; when ready to bake add 1 pint water or sufficient to form smooth batter that will run in a stream (not too thin) from pitcher; make griddle hot and cakes large as a saucer. When surface is covered with air holes it is time to turn cakes over; take off when sufficiently browned.

Wheat (or Flannel) Cakes.—1½ pints flour, 1 tablespoonful brown sugar, 1 teaspoonful salt, 2 heaping teaspoonfuls Royal Baking Powder, 2 eggs, 1½ pints milk. Sift together flour, sugar, salt, and powder; add beaten eggs and milk, mix into smooth batter, that will run in rather continuous stream from pitcher. Bake on good hot griddle, rich brown color, in cakes large as tea saucers. (It is not in good taste to have griddle cakes larger.) Serve with maple syrup.

Scotch Scones.—1 quart flour, 1 teaspoonful sugar, ½ teaspoonful salt, 2 teaspoonfuls Royal Baking Powder, 1 large tablespoonful lard, 2 eggs, nearly 1 pint milk. Sift together flour, sugar, salt, and powder; rub in lard cold; add beaten eggs and milk; mix into dough smooth and just consistent enough to handle. Flour the board, turn out dough, give it one or two quick kneadings to complete its smoothness; roll it out with rolling-pin to ½ inch in thickness, cut with sharp knife into squares larger than soda crackers, fold each in half to form three-cornered pieces. Bake on hot griddle 8 or 10 minutes; brown on both sides.

Apple Griddle Cakes.—Proceed as directed for *Squash or Pumpkin Griddle Cakes*, excepting this particular: Apples are usually thinner than the squash, consequently will not need so much milk.

Hominy Griddle Cakes.—Proceed as directed for *Rice Griddle Cakes*; serve with maple syrup.

Potato Scones.—6 potatoes, ½ pint Graham flour, ½ teaspoonful salt, ½ teaspoonful Royal Baking Powder, 1 tablespoonful butter. 1 cupful cream, 1 egg, ½ teaspoonful Royal Extract Cloves. Boil 6 moderately large potatoes, peeled, until very well done, drain off water, set them by fire with cover off to dry; mash exceedingly smooth, adding butter, egg and cream. Sift together Graham salt and powder, which add to potato preparation; when quite cold, add extract; mix into firm dough, which will require care in handling, as it is very short. Flour board with Graham, turn out dough, roll it to thickness of ½ inch, cut with sharp knife into oblong pieces—say length of soda crackers and ⅔ as wide. Bake on hot griddle, pricking them with fork to prevent blistering. Very light and delicate—to be eaten with butter.

Pancakes and Fritters.

APPLE FRITTERS.—4 large sound apples, peeled, cored, and cut each into 4 slices, ½ gill wine, 2 tablespoonfuls sugar, 1 teaspoonful Royal Extract Nutmeg. Place slices of apples in bowl with sugar, wine, and extract; cover with plate, set aside to steep two hours, then dip each slice in Common Batter, fry to light brown in plenty of lard made hot for the purpose; serve with sugar.

Banana Fritters.—5 bananas, stripped of skins and sliced in half lengthwise, Common Batter. Proceed as directed for Apple Fritters.

Custard Fritters.—½ pint milk, 5 eggs, ½ cupful sugar, 1 gill cream, Common Batter. Beat milk, cream, sugar, and eggs together; strain, put into small bowl, set in saucepan with boiling water to reach halfway up the sides of bowl; steam very gently until set, about 20 minutes; place on ice until cold; cut into pieces about 1½ inches long by 1 square; dip into common batter and fry, in plenty of hot lard, a deep fawn color; serve sprinkled with sugar.

Orange Fritters.—4 oranges, Common Batter. Peel oranges, taking off all the white pith without breaking into pulp, dividing each in 4 or 5 pieces through natural divisions of the orange; dip each piece into batter and fry deep yellow, in plenty of lard made hot for the purpose; serve on napkin with powdered sugar.

Rice Fritters.—1 cup rice, 1 pint milk, 3 eggs, 1 tablespoonful sugar, 2 tablespoonfuls butter. Boil rice in milk until soft and all the milk is absorbed, then remove, add yelks of eggs, sugar and butter; when cold add whites, whipped to dry froth; drop in spoonfuls in plenty of lard, made hot for the purpose, fry them deep buff color. Serve with Cream, Wine or Lemon Sauce.

Pancakes.—1 pint flour, 6 eggs, 1 saltspoonful salt, 1 teaspoonful Royal Baking Powder and milk to make a thin batter. Add the baking powder to the flour, beat the whites and yelks of eggs separately, add the yelks, salt, 2 cupfuls milk, then the whites and the flour alternately with milk, until the batter is of right consistency. Run 1 teaspoonful lard over the bottom of a hot frying-pan, pour in a large ladleful of batter, and fry quickly. Roll pancake up like a sheet of paper, lay upon a hot dish, put in more lard and fry another pancake. Keep hot over boiling water. Send ½ dozen to table at a time. Serve with sauce, jelly, or preserves.

Potato Pancakes.—12 large potatoes, 3 heaping tablespoonfuls flour, 1 teaspoonful Royal Baking Powder, ½ teaspoonful salt, 1 or 2 eggs, 2 teacupfuls boiling milk. The potatoes are peeled, washed and grated into a little cold water (which keeps them white), then strain off water and pour on boiling milk, stir in eggs, salt and flour mixed with the baking powder; if agreeable flavor with a little fine chopped onion, bake like any other pancakes, allowing a little more lard or butter. Serve with stewed or preserved fruit, especially with huckleberries.

French Pancakes.—Proceed as directed for English Pancakes; when all are done, spread each with any kind of preserves, roll up, sift over plenty sugar, glaze with red-hot poker.

Blackberry Fritters.—1 cupful blackberries. 1½ cupfuls Common Batter. Mix berries in batter in bowl, and drop by tablespoonfuls in plenty of lard made hot for the purpose; serve with Sauce. All berry fritters can be made as directed for the above.

Scotch Pancakes.—1 pint milk, 2 tablespoonfuls butter, 4 eggs, ⅔ cupful flour, 1 teaspoonful Royal Baking Powder, pinch salt. Sift flour, salt, and powder together, add milk, eggs, and butter melted, mix into thin batter; have small round frying-pan, with a little butter melted in it; pour in ½ cupful batter, turn pan round to cover it with the batter, place on hot fire to brown, then hold it up in front of fire, and the pancake will rise right up; spread each with marmalade or jelly; roll up, serve with sliced lemon and sugar.

English Pancakes.—1 pint milk, 2 eggs, 1 tablespoonful sugar, 1 cupful flour, 1 teaspoonful Royal Baking Powder, 1 cupful cream, pinch salt. Sift flour, salt, and powder together, add to it eggs beaten with sugar and diluted with milk and cream, mix into thin batter; have small round frying-pan, melt little butter in it, pour about half a cupful batter in it, turn pan round, that batter may cover the pan, put on hot fire; turn it and brown other side; butter each and roll it up. Sprinkle with powdered sugar.

Pastry.

Hints on Pastry.

FLOUR.—Should always be sifted just before you wish to use it.

ROYAL BAKING POWDER.—Should be thoroughly mixed with the flour dry.

BUTTER AND SUGAR FOR CAKE.—Should always be beaten to a cream.

EGGS.—Beat yelks until you can take up a spoonful; whip whites to stiff froth, and stir them into cake with the flour the last thing before putting cake into tins.

TO BOIL A PUDDING IN A BAG.—Dip bag (which should be made of thick cotton or linen) in hot water, and rub the inside with flour before putting in the pudding; when done dip bag in cold water and the pudding will turn out easily. Always put a plate on bottom of kettle to keep pudding from burning.

TO STEAM A PUDDING.—Put it into tin pan or earthen dish, tie a cloth over top and set it into a steamer; cover the steamer closely; allow a little longer time than you do for boiling.

TO MAKE CRUST FOR PIES, TARTS AND PUDDINGS.—Make pastry with clean, cold hands. Dip your hands in cold water (after washing them in hot water) before you begin, or your crust will not be good. Crust for company or the master's table is made with butter; for home or the servants, of clarified dripping or lard. Look to the oven; if it is too cold it will make your crust heavy, if too hot it will burn it. Try it, by baking a tiny piece of crust in it first. Make a little hole in top crust of meat pies to let out gas.

Apple sauce, ready for table use or pies, may be preserved by putting in hot jars and sealing at once. Remember cold fruit requires cold jars, hot fruit hot jars.

Weights and Measures.

1 cup, medium size, ½ pint or ½ pound.		
2 cups, medium size of sifted flour		
weigh	about	1 pound.
1 pint of sifted flour weighs	"	1 pound.
1 pint of white sugar weighs	"	1 pound.
2 tablespoonfuls of liquid	"	1 ounce.
8 teaspoonfuls of liquid	"	1 ounce.
1 gill of liquid (¼ lb.)	"	4 ounces.
1 pint of liquid (1 lb.)	"	16 ounces.

Cake.

CAKES.—An earthen basin is best for beating eggs or cake mixture. Cake should be beaten with a wooden spoon. It is well in making cake to beat the butter and powdered sugar to a light cream. In common cakes, when only a few eggs are used, beat them until you can take a spoonful up clear from strings. To ascertain whether a cake is baked enough, pass a small knife-blade through it; if not done enough, some of the unbaked dough will be found sticking to it; if done, it will come out clean.

Adelaide Cake.—1 cupful butter, 1½ cupfuls sugar, 4 eggs, 1 pint flour, 1 teaspoonful Royal Baking Powder, 1 cupful dried, stoned cherries, ½ cupful cream, 1 teaspoonful Royal Extract *Vanilla*. Rub butter and sugar to white, light cream; add eggs, 2 at a time, beating 5 minutes between each addition. Sift flour and powder together, add to butter, etc., with cherries, cream, and extract vanilla. Mix smoothly and gently into batter rather firm. Bake in paper-lined cake tin (fig. IX) 40 minutes in moderate, steady oven. Watch carefully; if getting too brown, protect with paper.

Almond Cake.—½ cupful butter, 2 cupfuls sugar, 4 eggs, ½ cupful almonds, blanched—by pouring water on them until skins easily slip off—and cut in fine shreds, ½ teaspoonful extract bitter almonds, 1 pint flour, 1½ teaspoonfuls Royal Baking Powder, 1 glass brandy, ½ cupful milk. Rub butter and sugar to smooth white cream; add eggs, 1 at a time, beating 3 or 4 minutes between each. Sift flour and powder together, add to butter, etc., with almonds, extract of bitter almonds, brandy, and milk; mix into smooth, medium batter, bake carefully in rather hot oven 20 minutes in a fluted mould (fig. I).

Angels' Food.—Dissolve ½ box gelatine in 1 quart milk; beat together yelks 3 eggs; 1 cupful of sugar, and juice of 1 lemon; stir into gelatine and milk, and let barely come to a boil; flavor with Royal Extract *Vanilla*. When nearly cold, whip whites of eggs to stiff froth, and stir through custard. Pour into moulds and set away to cool.

Apple Jelly Cake.—1 cupful butter, 2 cupfuls sugar, 4 eggs, 3 cupfuls flour, 1½ teaspoonfuls Royal Baking Powder, 1 cupful milk, 6 apples, 6 ounces sugar, 1 teaspoonful butter. Rub together butter and sugar to fine light, white cream, add eggs 2 at a time, beating 10 minutes between each addition. Sift flour and Royal Baking Powder together, add to butter, etc., with milk, and mix into rather thin batter. Bake in jelly cake tins carefully greased. Meanwhile have apples peeled and sliced, put on fire with sugar; when tender remove, rub through fine sieve, and add butter. When cold use to spread between layers. Cover cake plentifully with sugar, sifted over top.

Bath Buns.—Half cupful butter, 1½ cupfuls sugar, 2 eggs, 1½ teaspoonfuls Royal Baking Powder, ½ cupful candied lemon peel, cut in small thin slices, 1½ pints flour, ½ pint milk. Rub the butter and sugar to a smooth, light cream; add the eggs, beat a few minutes longer; then add the flour, with the powder sifted in it, the lemon peel and milk. Mix into a moderately firm batter. Lay greased muffin rings on a greased baking tin (fig. XIV), and put a large spoonful into each. Sift sugar on them, and bake 15 minutes in a hot oven.

Chocolate Cake.—Proceed as directed for *Cream Cake No. 2*, spreading between the layers of cake the following: Chocolate cream, 1 pint milk, 1 tablespoonful good butter, 1 cup sugar, one-half cup grated chocolate. 2 teaspoonfuls corn starch, yelks 3 eggs, 1 teaspoonful Royal Extract *Vanilla*. Bring the milk to boil, stir in the chocolate, the sugar, and corn starch, boil 5 minutes; take from the fire, add the egg yelks, stirring rapidly the while; return to the fire to set the eggs, add the butter cool, and then add the vanilla.

Caraway Cake.—Proceed as directed for *Currant Cake*, substituting 2 tablespoonfuls caraway seeds for the currants.

Chocolate Cream (Glace).—Proceed as for *Chocolate Cake* and finish by glazing with the following: Set on the fire 1 gill of water, 1½ cupfuls sugar, ½ cup grated chocolate in a small saucepan; boil until it gets thick and looks velvety; take off the fire, and add the whites of 2 eggs, without beating; use it hot, covering the top and sides of the cake. As it cools it grows firm.

Cocoanut Cake.—Proceed as directed for *Cream Cake No. 2*, spreading between the layers grated cocoanut and *Pastry Cream* in proportion of a cupful of the former to two of the latter. Sift sugar over the top.

Citron Cake.—1½ cupfuls butter, 2 cupfuls sugar, 6 eggs, 1 teaspoonful Royal Baking Powder, 1 pint flour, 1 cupful citron, cut in thin large slices, 1 teaspoonful Royal Extract *Nutmeg*. Rub the butter and sugar to a smooth, light cream, add the eggs, 2 at a time, beating 5 minutes between each addition. Sift the flour and powder together, which add to the butter, etc., with the citron and extract nutmeg. Mix into a firm batter, and bake carefully in paper lined shallow flat cake pan (fig. XIII), in a moderate oven, 50 minutes.

Cocoanut Meringue Cake.—Proceed as directed for *Cream Cake No. 2*; when finished cover the top and side with a meringue as follows: Whites of 6 eggs, 1 cupful sugar, 1 cup of cocoanut. Beat the whites to a dry froth, then add the sugar mixed with the cocoanut all at once; stir very gently, but mix thoroughly together; use as directed; sift sugar over. When the cake is masked, put in a very slow oven until a fine fawn color.

Coffee Cake.—1 cupful very strong coffee, 1 cupful butter, 2 cupfuls sugar, 3 eggs, 1½ pints flour, 1½ teaspoonfuls Royal Baking Powder, 1 cupful stoned raisins, cut in two, ½ cupful chopped citron, 10 drops each Royal Extract *Allspice* and *Nutmeg*, and ½ cupful milk. Rub the butter and sugar to a white cream; add the eggs, 1 at a time, beating 3 or 4 minutes between each. Sift together flour and powder, which add to the butter, etc., with the coffee, raisins, citron, milk, and extracts. Mix into a smooth batter. Bake in paper lined cake tin (fig. IX), in a hot oven 50 minutes.

Composition Cake.—1 cupful butter, 2½ cupfuls sugar, 4 eggs, 2 teaspoonfuls Royal Baking Powder, 1 quart flour, 1½ cupfuls raisins, stoned and chopped, 1½ cupfuls currants, washed and picked, 1 teaspoonful each Royal Extract *Cinnamon* and *Nutmeg*, 1 cup milk. Rub the butter and sugar to a thick, white cream; add the eggs, 1 at a time, beating a few minutes between each. Sift the flour with the powder, which add to the butter, etc., the raisins, currants, milk, and extract; mix into a smooth batter. Bake in paper lined shallow, flat cake pan (fig. XIII), in a moderate oven 1 hour. When nearly cold, strip off the paper and ice the bottom with *Clear Icing*.

Cream Cakes, No. 1 (Ecliars a la Creme).—10 eggs, ½ cupful butter, ¾ lb. flour, 1 pint water, 1½ pints milk, 3 large tablespoonfuls corn starch, 2 cupfuls sugar, yelks 5 eggs, 1 large tablespoonful good butter, and 2 teaspoonfuls Royal Extract *Vanilla*. Set the water on the fire in a stewpan with the butter; as soon as it boils, stir in the sifted flour with a wooden spoon; stir vigorously until it leaves the bottom and sides of the stewpan when removed from the fire, and beat in the eggs, one at a time. Place this batter in a pointed canvas bag, having a nozzle at the small end. Press out the batter in the shape of fingers, on a greased baking-tin, a little distance apart. Bake in a steady brick oven 20 minutes. When cold, cut the sides and fill with the following:

PASTRY CREAM.

Bring the milk to boil with the sugar; add the starch dissolved in little water; as soon as it reboils, take from the fire; beat in the egg yelks; return to the fire two minutes to set the eggs; add the extract and butter. When cold use as directed.

Crullers. — 1 quart flour, ½ cupful lard, ½ cupful butter, 1 cupful sugar, 1½ teaspoonfuls Royal Baking Powder, ¾ pint milk, 2 eggs, 1 teaspoonful Royal Extract *Nutmeg*. Sift the flour, sugar, and powder together; rub in the lard and butter; add the beaten eggs, extract, and milk. Mix into a smooth dough, and just soft enough to handle conveniently. Roll out with the rolling pin on a well floured board; cut into strips about ½ inch square, twist in different shapes, and fry to a light brown color in plenty hot lard. Serve with sifted sugar.

Currant Jelly Cake. — Proceed as directed for *Cream Cake No. 2*, substituting *Currant Jelly* for the *Pastry Cream*.

Confederate Cake. — 2 cupfuls butter, 2 cupfuls sugar, 10 eggs, ½ teaspoonful Royal Baking Powder, 1½ pints flour. Rub the butter and sugar to a light, white cream; add the eggs, 2 at a time, beating 10 minutes between the two first additions, and five minutes between the rest. Add the flour sifted with the powder, and mix into a smooth medium batter. Bake very carefully in rather small paper lined tins (fig. XII), in a moderate oven, 35 to 40 minutes.

Cream Cake No. 2. — ¾ cupful butter, 2 cups sugar, 1½ pints flour, 5 eggs, 1 teaspoonful Royal Baking Powder, 1 cupful milk. Rub the butter and sugar to a white, light cream; add the eggs, 2 at a time, beating 5 minutes between each addition. Sift the flour with the powder, which add to the butter, etc., and the milk. Mix into rather thin batter, and bake in jelly cake tins well greased, in hot oven 15 minutes. When cold spread *Pastry Cream* between each layer, and ice the top with *Clear Icing*. (See *Pastry Cream* page 7.)

Cup Cake. — 1 cupful butter, 2 cupfuls sugar, 4 eggs, 1 teaspoonful Royal Baking Powder, 3 cupfuls flour, 20 drops Royal Extract *Bitter Almonds*. Rub the butter and sugar to a cream; add the eggs, 2 at a time, beating it five minutes between each addition. Sift together the flour and powder, which add to the butter, etc., with the extract. Mix into a smooth, medium batter; bake in well greased cups or muffin pans (fig. VII), in a rather hot oven 20 minutes.

Currant Cake. — 1 cupful butter, 1 cupful sugar, 4 eggs, 1 teaspoonful Royal Baking Powder, 1 pint flour, 1½ cupfuls currants, washed and picked, 2 teaspoonfuls Royal Extract of *Cinnamon*, and 1 teaspoonful Royal Extract *Lemon*. Rub the butter and sugar to a white, light cream; add the eggs, one at a time, beating a few minutes between each; add the flour sifted with the powder, the currants, and the extracts. Mix into a medium batter. Bake in paper lined cake tin (fig. IX), 50 minutes in a moderate oven.

Currant Cake (English). — 1½ cupfuls butter, 2 cupfuls sugar, 7 eggs, 1 teaspoonful Royal Baking Powder, ½ cupful citron, in small thin slices, the rind of an orange, peeled very thin, and cut in shreds, 2 cupfuls currants, washed and picked, 1½ pints flour, 1 teaspoonful Royal Extract *Nutmeg*. Rub the butter and sugar to a white, light cream; add the eggs, 2 at a time, beating 5 minutes between each addition. Sift the flour and the powder together; add it to the butter, etc., with the citron, orange peel, currants, and the extract. Bake in a thickly paper lined tin (fig. XIII), 1 hour 25 minutes, in a moderate oven.

Dundee Cake. — 2 cupfuls butter, 1½ cupfuls sugar, 8 eggs, 1½ pints flour, 1 teaspoonful Royal Baking Powder, ½ lemon peel cut in thin small slices, 1 cupful washed, picked, dried currants, 1½ cupfuls sultana raisins, 1 teaspoonful each Royal Extract *Nutmeg*, *Cloves*, and *Vanilla*, ½ cupful cream, 1 cupful almonds, if at hand. Rub the butter and sugar to a white, light cream; add the eggs, 2 at a time, beating 5 minutes between each addition; add the flour, sifted with the powder, the lemon peel, currants, raisins, extracts, and the milk; mix into a rather firm batter, pour into a paper lined, shallow, square, cake pan (fig. XIII), chop the almonds coarsely, sprinkle over the top, and bake in a moderate oven 1½ hours.

Duchesse Cake. — 1½ cupfuls butter, 1 cupful sugar, 6 eggs, 1 teaspoonful Royal Baking Powder, 1 pint flour, 1 teaspoonful Royal Extract *Cinnamon*. Rub the butter and sugar to a light cream; add the eggs, 2 at a time, beating 10 minutes between each addition. Sift together flour and powder, add to the butter, etc., with the extract; mix into a medium thick batter, and bake in small, shallow, square pans (fig. XII), lined with thin white paper, in a steady oven 30 minutes. When they are taken from the oven, ice them.

Soft Gingerbread. — ½ cupful butter, 2 cupfuls molasses, 1 cupful sugar, 4 cupfuls flour, 1 cupful milk, 4 eggs, 1 teaspoonful Royal Baking Powder, ginger and cloves to taste.

Doughnuts. — ½ cupful butter, 1 cupful sugar, 1½ pints flour, 1½ teaspoonfuls Royal Baking Powder, 1 egg, 1½ cupfuls milk, 1 teaspoonful Royal Extract *Nutmeg*. Rub the butter, sugar, and egg together smooth. Sift the flour and powder together, add it to the butter, the milk, etc. Mix into a soft dough; well flour the board, roll out the dough to ½ inch in thickness, cut out with large biscuit cutter, and fry to a light brown in plenty of lard made hot for the purpose. Serve with sifted sugar over them.

Drop Cake. — 1 cupful butter, ½ cupful sugar, 2 eggs, 1 small teaspoonful Royal Baking Powder, 1 pint flour, 1 cupful washed and picked currants, 1 teaspoonful each Royal Extract *Nutmeg* and *Lemon*, ½ cupful milk. Rub the butter and sugar to a white light cream; add the eggs, beat 10 minutes longer; add the flour and powder sifted together, the milk and extracts. Mix into a rather firm batter, and drop with a spoon on a greased baking tin (fig. XIV); bake in a quick oven 10 minutes.

Dried Apple Cake. — Soak 3 cups dried apples in warm water over night, drain off the water through a sieve, chop the apples slightly, then simmer them for 2 hours in 3 cups molasses, then add 2 eggs, 1 cup sugar, 1 cup sweet milk or water, then ¼ cup butter or lard, flour to make a stiff batter, 2 heaping teaspoonfuls baking powder in flour. Cinnamon, cloves, nutmeg, etc., to taste. Raisins added improve the cake very much.

Election Cake. — 1½ cupfuls butter, 2 cupfuls sugar, 1½ pints flour, 3 eggs, 1½ teaspoonfuls Royal Baking Powder, 2 cupfuls raisins, stoned, 1 cupful currants, washed and picked, ½ cupful chopped citron, ½ lemon peel chopped, ½ cupful almonds, blanched and cut in shreds, 20 drops each Royal Extract of *Bitter Almonds* and *Vanilla*, 1 cupful milk. Rub the butter and sugar to a white, light cream; add the eggs, beating a while longer, the flour sifted with the powder, raisins, citron, currants, lemon peel, almonds, extracts, and milk; mix into a consistent batter; put in a paper lined tin (fig. XIII), and bake in a moderate oven 1½ hours.

French Cake. — 1½ cupfuls butter, 2 cupfuls sugar, 12 eggs, 1 quart flour, ½ teaspoonful Royal Baking Powder, 1 gill each of cream, wine, and brandy, 20 drops each Royal Extract *Bitter Almonds*, and *Nutmeg*, 1½ cupful raisins, stoned, ½ cupful almonds, blanched, 1 cupful chopped citron. Rub butter and sugar to a white, light cream; add the eggs, 2 at a time, beating 10 minutes between the 3 first additions, and 5 minutes between the rest; add the flour, sifted with the powder, raisins, almonds, citron, extracts, cream, wine, and brandy. Mix into a smooth, consistent batter; bake in a thickly paper lined cake pan (fig. XIII), in a steady oven 2 hours.

Graham Cup Cake. — ¾ cupful butter, 1 cupful sugar, ½ cupful cream, 2 eggs, 2 cupfuls Graham flour, 1 teaspoonful Royal Baking Powder, 1 teaspoonful Royal Extract *Lemon*. Rub the butter and sugar to a light, white cream; add the eggs, 1 at a time, beating a few minutes between each; sift the Graham and powder together, which add to the butter, etc., the cream, and extract; mix into a moderately thin batter, bake in well greased cups, or muffin pans (fig. VII), 20 minutes in a moderate, steady oven.

THE ROYAL BAKING POWDER IS ABSOLUTELY PURE.

Ginger Sponge Cake.—2 cupfuls brown sugar, 4 eggs, 1 pint flour, two-thirds cup water, 1½ teaspoonfuls Royal Baking Powder, 1 tablespoonful Royal Extract *Ginger*, 1 teaspoonful Royal Extract *Lemon*. Beat the eggs and sugar together for 10 minutes; add the water, the flour sifted with the powder, and the extracts; mix into a smooth sponge, and bake in quick oven 30 minutes.

Gingerbread.—1 cupful brown sugar, and 1 tablespoonful butter, stirred to a cream; add 1 cupful New Orleans molasses, and mix well; stir dry 2 teaspoonfuls Royal Baking Powder in 2½ cupfuls flour; put in ginger or spice to taste. Bake in 1 large loaf 1 hour, or 2 small loaves ½ hour.

Ginger Cake.—¾ cupful butter, 2 cupfuls sugar, 4 eggs, 1½ teaspoonfuls Royal Baking Powder, 1½ pints flour, 1 cupful milk, 1 tablespoonful Royal Extract *Ginger*. Rub the butter and sugar to a light cream; add the eggs, two at a time, beating 5 minutes between; add the flour, sifted with the powder, the milk and extract; mix into a smooth batter; bake in a cake tin (fig. IX), in rather hot oven 40 minutes.

Ginger Snaps.—½ cupful lard, ½ cupful butter, 1 large cupful brown sugar, 1 cupful water, 1 tablespoonful Royal Extract *Ginger*, 1 teaspoonful each Royal Extract *Cinnamon* and *Cloves*, 1 quart flour, 1½ teaspoonfuls Royal Baking Powder. Rub to a smooth paste the lard, butter and sugar; then rub it into the flour and powder sifted together. Mix into a firm dough with the flour and extracts. Roll out the dough thin on a floured board, cut out with a round biscuit cutter, and bake on greased pan (fig. XIV), in a hot, steady oven 8 minutes.

Gold Cake.—¾ cupful butter, 2 cupfuls sugar, yelks of 10 eggs, 1½ pints flour, 2 teaspoonfuls Royal Baking Powder, 1 cupful thin cream, one teaspoonful each Royal Extract *Lemon* and *Nutmeg*. Rub the butter and sugar to a white cream; add the yelks, three at a time, beating a little between each addition; add the flour sifted with the powder, the thin cream and the extracts; mix into a pretty firm batter; bake in a paper-lined cake tin (fig. IX), in a steady oven, 50 minutes.

Honey Cake.—½ cupful butter, 1 cupful sugar, 1 cupful honey, 1 pint flour, 1 teaspoonful Royal Baking Powder, 2 eggs, 1 teaspoonful caraway seeds. Mix the honey with the sugar; add the butter melted, the eggs slightly beaten, the flour, sifted with the powder, and the seeds; mix into a smooth batter of the consistency of *Sponge Cake*, and bake in a fairly hot oven 35 minutes.

Jelly Cake.—Beat 3 eggs well, whites and yelks separately; take a cupful of fine white sugar and beat in well with yelks, and cupful sifted flour, stirred in gently; then stir in the whites, a little at a time, teaspoonful Royal Baking Powder and 1 tablespoonful milk; pour it into 3 jelly cake plates and bake from 5 to 10 minutes in a well-heated oven; when cold spread with currant jelly, place each layer on top of the other, and sift powdered sugar on top.

Jelly Cake.—*See Currant Jelly Cake.*

Jumbles No. 1.—1 cupful butter, 1 cupful sugar, 4 eggs, 2 cupfuls flour, ½ teaspoonful Royal Baking Powder. Rub together the butter and sugar; add the beaten eggs and flour, sifted with the powder; flour the board, roll out the dough rather thin, cut with jumble cutter, or any you may have; roll in sugar, lay out on greased tin (fig. XIII); bake in fairly hot oven 10 minutes.

Jumbles No. 2.—1½ cupfuls butter, 2 cupfuls sugar, 6 eggs, 1½ pints flour, ½ cupful corn starch, 1 teaspoonful Royal Baking Powder, 1 teaspoonful Royal Extract *Lemon*, ½ cupful chopped peanuts, mixed with ½ cupful granulated sugar. Beat the butter and sugar smooth; add the beaten eggs, the flour, corn starch, and powder, sifted together, and the extract; flour the board, roll out the dough rather thin, cut out with biscuit cutter, roll in the chopped peanuts and sugar, lay on greased baking tin (fig. XIII); bake in rather hot oven 8 to 10 minutes.

Lemon Cake No. 1.—1 cupful butter, 2 cupfuls sugar, 7 eggs, 1½ pints flour, 1 teaspoonful Royal Baking Powder, 1 teaspoonful Royal Extract of *Lemon*. Rub to a light cream the butter and sugar; add the eggs, 2 at a time, beating 5 minutes between each addition; add the flour, sifted with the powder, and the extract; mix into a medium batter; bake in paper-lined tin (fig. XIII), in a moderate oven, 40 minutes.

Lemon Cake No. 2.—Proceed as directed for *Cream Cake (Eclairs à la Crême)*, flavoring the *Pastry Cream* with 1 teaspoonful Royal Extract *Lemon*.

Lady Cake.—1½ cupfuls butter, 3 cupfuls sugar, whites 8 eggs, 1 pint flour, ½ teaspoonful Royal Baking Powder, 1 cupful milk, 20 drops Royal Extract *Bitter Almonds*. Rub the butter and sugar to a cream; add the flour, sifted with the powder, milk and extract; mix into a smooth batter; then gently mix the 8 egg whites, whipped to a dry froth; when thoroughly mixed, put into a shallow cake pan (fig. XIII), papered, and bake carefully in steady oven 40 minutes. When cool, ice the bottom and sides with *White Icing*.

Lafayette Cake.—Proceed as directed for *Gateaux à la Meniere*, substituting *Chocolate Cream* for the fruit, jam or jelly, and ice the top with *Transparent Icing*, colored pink with a few drops of extract of cochineal. Strew the top of the icing with finely chopped citron.

Lunch Cake (Boston).—2 cupfuls butter, 2 cupfuls sugar, 1½ pints flour, 1 teaspoonful Royal Baking Powder, 6 eggs, 1 gill wine, 1 teaspoonful each Royal Extract *Rose*, *Cinnamon* and *Nutmeg*. Rub the butter and sugar to a very light cream; add the eggs, 2 at a time, beating 5 minutes between each addition; add the flour, sifted with the powder, wine, extracts; mix into a smooth batter, put into a thickly papered, shallow cake pan (fig. XIII), and bake in moderate oven 1¼ hours. When cold, ice the bottom and sides with *White Icing*.

Marbled Cake.—This is made in separate batters, a dark and a light one. For the dark one, take ½ cupful butter, 1 cupful brown sugar, 2½ cupfuls flour, 1 teaspoonful Royal Baking Powder, 4 yelks of eggs, ½ cupful milk, 1 teaspoonful each Royal Extract *Cinnamon*, *Cloves* and *Allspice*. For the light one take ½ cupful butter, 1 cupful sugar, 2½ cupfuls flour, 1 teaspoonful Royal Baking Powder, whites of 4 eggs, ½ cupful milk, 1 teaspoonful Royal Extract *Lemon*. Both batters are made by rubbing the butter and sugar to a cream; adding the eggs, beat a few minutes, then add the flour, sifted with the powder, the extracts and milk, and mix into smooth batter, rather firm. Have a paper-lined tin (fig. IX); with a spoon drop the two batters alternately into it, and bake in a rather quick oven 35 minutes.

Chocolate Cream Cake.—1½ pounds each butter, sugar and flour, 18 eggs. Beat the yelks separate with sugar and butter. Beat the whites separately, and add to above. To ½ of the dough mix ¼ pound chocolate, and bake of each part (the dark and light) 6 cakes. In place of jelly put ¾ pint of cream and yelks of 8 eggs. Sugar to taste, flavor with Royal Extract *Vanilla*. Put on fire and stir until it thickens, then put between the cakes.

Mountain Cake.—1 cupful butter, 2½ cupfuls sugar, 3 whole eggs, and 3 yelks, 1 pint flour, 1½ teaspoonfuls Royal Baking Powder, 1 cupful milk, 1 teaspoonful Royal Extract *Vanilla*, 1 cupful red currant jelly, 2 cupfuls sugar, 3 whites eggs. Rub the butter and sugar to a light white cream; add the eggs 1 at a time, and the yelks all at once, beating 5 minutes between each addition; add the flour sifted with the powder, the milk and extract; mix the whole into a smooth light batter; put in a shallow, square pan (fig. XIII), bake in a moderate oven 40 minutes. When cold, cover the top with the following: Beat up the jelly with the whites of eggs and sugar, until light and stiff, then use as directed.

Molasses Cake.—1 cupful butter, 1 cupful brown sugar, ½ cupful molasses, 1 cupful milk, 1½ pints flour, 1½ teaspoonfuls Royal Baking Powder, 1 egg. Rub smooth the butter and sugar; add the milk, egg and molasses, stir in the flour, sifted with the powder; mix into a consistent batter, and bake in cake tin (fig. IX), 40 minutes.

Orange Cake No. 1.—½ cupful butter, 2 cupfuls sugar, 5 eggs, 1 pint flour, 1½ teaspoonfuls Royal Baking Powder, 1 teaspoonful Royal Extract *Orange*, 1 cupful milk. Rub the butter and sugar to a cream; add the eggs, 2 at a time, beating 5 minutes between each addition; add the flour, sifted with the powder; the milk and extract; mix into a smooth, fine batter, put in a paper lined cake tin (fig. IX), and bake in a moderate oven 30 minutes. When cool, cover the top with the following preparation: Whip the whites of 3 eggs to a dry froth; then carefully mix in 4 cups sugar, the juice, grated rind and soft pulp, free of white pith and seeds, of 2 sour oranges.

Orange Cake No. 2. Proceed as directed for *Cream Cake No. 2*, substituting orange marmalade for the *Pastry Cream*.

Apple Butter Cake. 2 cups brown sugar, 4 eggs, 1 pint flour, ⅔ cup of water, 1½ teaspoonfuls of Royal Baking Powder, 1 tablespoonful of Royal Extract of *Ginger*, 1 teaspoonful of Royal Extract of *Lemon*. Beat the eggs and sugar together for 10 minutes, add the water, the flour, sifted with the powder, and the extracts. Mix into a smooth batter, and bake in jelly tins, and when done lay the cakes together, with sweet apple butter between, and ice.

Delicious Little Cakes can be made by making a rich jumble paste rolling out in any desired shape; cut some paste in thick, narrow strips and lay around your cakes so as to form a deep cup-like edge; place on a well-buttered tin and bake. When done, fill with iced fruit, prepared as follows: Take rich, ripe peaches (canned ones will do if fine and well drained from all juice), cut in halves; plums, strawberries, pineapples cut in squares, or small triangles, or any other available fruit, and dip in the white of an egg that has been very slightly beaten and then in pulverized sugar, and lay in the centre of your cakes.

Nut Cake.—½ cupful butter, 1½ cupfuls sugar, 3 eggs, 2½ cupfuls flour, 1½ teaspoonfuls Royal Baking Powder, ½ cup milk, 1 cupful of any meats of nuts preferred or at hand. Rub the butter and sugar to a light, white cream; add the eggs, beaten a little, then the flour, sifted with the powder; mix with the milk and nuts into a rather firm batter, and bake in a paper lined tin (fig. IX), in a steady oven 35 minutes.

Pound Cake. 1½ cupfuls butter, 2 cupfuls sugar, 7 eggs, 1½ pints flour, 1 teaspoonful Royal Baking Powder, 1 teaspoonful Royal Extract *Nutmeg*. Rub the butter and sugar to a white, light cream; add 3 of the eggs, 1 at a time, and the rest 2 at a time, beating 5 minutes between each addition; add the flour, sifted with the powder; add the extract; mix into a smooth, medium batter, and bake in a paper lined cake tin (fig. XIII), in a steady oven, 50 minutes.

Rice Cakes.—½ cupful butter, 2 cupfuls sugar, 4 eggs, 1½ cups rice flour, 1½ cups flour, 1 teaspoonful Royal Baking Powder, ½ cup cream, 1 teaspoonful Royal Extract *Lemon*. Beat the eggs and sugar together 10 minutes; add the butter, melted; sift together flour, rice flour, and the powder, which add to the eggs, etc., with the cream and the extract; mix into a thin batter, and bake in patty pans, well greased, in a hot oven, 10 minutes.

Pond Lily Cake.—1 cup of butter, 1½ cups of sugar, whites of 5 eggs, 1½ pints flour, 1½ teaspoonfuls Royal Baking Powder, 1 cup milk; flavor with Royal Extract *Peach* and a few drops of Royal Extract *Rose*. Bake in 2 cakes, in very deep jelly or sponge tins, and when done put together with freshly grated cocoanut and pulverized sugar between and on top of the cakes, and ice with *Clear Icing*.

Peach Blossom Cake.—1 cup of pulverized sugar, ½ cup butter, stirred together until it looks like thick cream, 2 teaspoonfuls of Royal Baking Powder, ½ teacupful of sweet milk; beat the whites of 3 eggs, and add to a teacupful of flour mixed with the baking powder; stir and add ½ teaspoonful of corn starch. Flavor strongly with Royal Extract *Peach*. Bake in 2 square sponge tins in moderately quick oven, and when done sandwich with finely grated cocoanut and pink sugar. Frost with *Clear Icing*, and sprinkle this with pulverized pink sugar.

Queen Cake.—2 cupfuls butter, 2½ cupfuls sugar, 1½ pints flour, 8 eggs, ½ teaspoonful Royal Baking Powder, 1 wineglassful each wine, brandy, and cream, ½ teaspoonful each Royal Extract *Nutmeg*, *Rose* and *Lemon*, 1 cupful dried currants, washed and picked, 1 cupful raisins, stoned and cut in two, 1 cupful citron, cut in small, thin slices. Rub the butter and sugar to a very light cream; add the eggs, 2 at a time, beating 5 minutes between each addition; add the flour, sifted with the powder, the raisins, currants, wine, brandy, cream, citron and extracts; mix into a batter, and bake carefully in a papered cake tin (fig. XIII), in a moderately steady oven, 1½ hours.

Reception Cake.—2 cupfuls butter, 2 cupfuls sugar, 10 eggs, 1 quart flour, 1 teaspoonful Royal Baking Powder, 2 cupfuls currants, washed and picked, 1 cupful citron, in thin, small slices, ½ orange rind, peeled very thin and cut small, ½ cupful almonds, blanched by pouring boiling water on them until the skins slip off easily—and cut in shreds, 1 teaspoonful each Royal Extract *Allspice* and *Cinnamon*. Rub the butter and sugar to a white, light cream; add the eggs, 2 at a time, beating 5 minutes between each addition; add the flour sifted with the powder, currants, citron, orange peel, almonds, and extracts; mix carefully into a rather soft batter; put it into a paper lined shallow cake tin (fig. XIII), using 3 thicknesses of stout paper; bake it carefully in a moderate, steady oven 2¼ hours.

Sponge Cake.—2 cupfuls sugar, 7 eggs, 1 cup flour, 1 teaspoonful Royal Baking Powder, a pinch salt, 1 teaspoonful Royal Extract *Lemon*. Whip sugar and eggs together until thick and white; add flour, sifted with powder, and salt, and the extract; mix together quickly, bake in tin (fig. XII), lined with buttered paper, in hot oven, 35 minutes.

Sponge Cake (Almond).—1½ cupfuls sugar (cut), 8 eggs, 1½ cupfuls flour, ½ teaspoonful Royal Baking Powder, 1 teaspoonful Royal Extract *Bitter Almonds*. Boil sugar in 1½ gills of water until, taking some up on end of spoon handle and cooling in water, it breaks brittle, when at once pour it on the eggs, previously whipped 10 minutes; continue the whipping 20 minutes longer; add flour, sifted with powder, and extract; bake in well buttered cake mould (fig. I), in quick oven, 30 minutes.

Sponge Cake (Berwick).—6 eggs, 3 cupfuls sugar, 4 cupfuls flour, 2 teaspoonfuls Royal Baking Powder, 1 cupful cold water, pinch salt, 1 teaspoonful Royal Extract *Lemon*. Beat eggs and sugar together 5 minutes; add flour, sifted with salt and powder, water, and extract; bake in shallow square cake pan (fig. XIII), in quick, steady oven, 35 minutes; when removed from oven, ice it with *Clear Icing*.

Tea Cake No. 1.—½ cupful butter, 1½ cupfuls sugar, 1½ pints flour, 1½ teaspoonfuls Royal Baking Powder, 1 teaspoonful Royal Extract *Nutmeg*. Sift flour, sugar, and powder together; rub in butter cold; add milk and extract; mix into dough soft enough to handle easily; flour the board, roll out dough to the thickness of ½ inch; cut out with biscuit cutter; lay on greased baking tin (fig. XIII), wash over with milk; bake in hot oven 20 minutes.

Tea Cake No. 2.—Proceed as directed for *Coffee Cake*, substituting tea for coffee.

Royal Cookies. — 1 cupful butter, 2 cupfuls sugar, 5 eggs, 1½ pints flour, ½ teaspoonful Royal Baking Powder, 1 cup milk. Mix butter, sugar and eggs smooth ; add flour, sifted with powder, and milk ; mix into dough, soft enough to handle conveniently ; flour the board, roll out dough, thin ; cut out with biscuit cutter ; lay on greased baking tin, bake in hot oven 5 or 6 minutes.

Spice Cake. — 1 cupful butter, 1 cupful brown sugar, 1 pint flour, 2 teaspoonfuls Royal Baking Powder, 1 teaspoonful each caraway and coriander seeds, 1 teaspoonful each Royal Extract *Nutmeg, Cinnamon* and *Ginger*, 1 cupful milk. Sift flour, sugar and powder together ; rub in butter ; add milk, seeds, and extracts ; mix smooth into batter of medium thickness ; fill greased patié pans ⅔ full ; bake in hot oven, 8 or 10 minutes.

Spencer Cakes. — 2 cupfuls sugar, 8 eggs, 1½ pints flour, 1 teaspoonful Royal Baking Powder, 2 tablespoonfuls coriander seed, 1 teaspoonful Royal Extract *Lemon*. Beat eggs and sugar together, until they get thick and white ; add flour, sifted with powder, the seed, and extract ; mix into rather thick sponge ; drop in spoonfuls on greased tin (fig. XIV), bake in hot oven 5 or 6 minutes.

Scotch Cake. — 1½ cupfuls butter, 2½ cupfuls sugar, 8 eggs, 1½ pints flour, ½ teaspoonful Royal Baking Powder, 3 cupfuls raisins, stoned, 1 tablespoonful Royal Extract *Lemon*. Rub butter and sugar to light, white cream ; add eggs, 2 at a time, beating 5 minutes between each addition ; add flour, sifted with powder, raisins, and extract ; mix into smooth batter ; put into paper lined, square, shallow cake pan (fig. XIII), bake in moderate oven 1 hour.

Shrewsbury Cake. — 1 cupful butter, 3 cupfuls sugar, 1½ pints flour, 3 eggs, 1 teaspoonful Royal Baking Powder, 1 cupful milk, 1 teaspoonful Royal Extract *Rose*. Rub butter and sugar to smooth white cream ; add eggs, 1 at a time, beating 5 minutes between each ; add flour, sifted with powder, and extract ; mix into medium batter ; bake in cake mould (fig. I), well and carefully greased, in quick oven, 40 minutes.

Silver Cake. — Proceed as directed for *Gold Cake*, substituting whites of eggs for the yelks.

Vanilla Cake. — 1½ cupfuls butter, 2 cupfuls sugar, 6 yelks eggs, 1 pint flour, 1½ teaspoonfuls Royal Baking Powder, 1 cupful cream, 1 teaspoonful Royal Extract *Vanilla*. Rub butter and sugar to very light cream ; add egg yelks and cream, flour, sifted with powder, and extract ; mix into smooth, rather firm batter ; bake in shallow square pan (fig XIII), in fairly hot oven, 35 minutes.

Washington Cake (St. Louis, 1780). — 2 cupfuls butter, 3 cupfuls sugar, 4 cupfuls flour, 2 teaspoonfuls Royal Baking Powder, 5 eggs, 1 cupful milk, 1 cupful stoned raisins, ½ cupful washed and picked currants, ¼ cupful chopped citron, 1 teaspoonful each Royal Extract *Nutmeg* and *Cinnamon*. Rub butter and sugar to white, light cream ; add beaten eggs gradually, the flour, sifted with powder, milk, raisins, currants, citron, and extracts ; mix into smooth, medium batter ; bake in shallow, square cake pan (fig. XIII), in rather quick, steady oven, 1½ hours ; when cold ice with *White Icing*.

Webster Cake. — 1 cupful butter, 3 cupfuls sugar, 2 eggs, 5 cupfuls flour, 1 teaspoonful Royal Baking Powder, 2 cupfuls raisins, seeded, 1 teaspoonful each Royal Extract *Bitter Almonds* and *Vanilla*, 1½ cupfuls milk. Rub butter, sugar, and eggs smooth ; add flour sifted with powder, raisins, milk and extracts ; mix into medium batter ; bake in cake mould (fig. I), in quick, steady oven, 45 minutes.

Wild Rose Cake. — Make the dough after the recipe given for *Pond Lily Cake*, flavoring with Royal Rose and *Strawberry* instead of peach. Bake in 2 inch-deep jelly tins, and sandwich with pink icing, and the same on top. (Made by substituting finely pulverized pink sugar for white.) When you have put the last layer of pink icing on top, sift very lightly over the top granulated white sugar.

Wine Cake. — 1½ cupfuls butter, 2 cupfuls sugar, 2 cupfuls flour, ½ teaspoonful Royal Baking Powder, 1 gill wine, 3 eggs. Rub butter and sugar to light cream, add eggs, 1 at a time, beating 5 minutes between each ; add flour, sifted with powder, and wine ; mix into medium firm batter ; bake in shallow, square cake pan (fig. XIII), in moderate oven, 40 minutes ; when taken from oven carefully ice with *Transparent Icing*.

Wedding (or Bride) Cake. — 6 cupfuls butter, 4 cupfuls sugar, 16 eggs, 3 pints flour, 6 cupfuls currants, washed, dried, and picked, 3 cupfuls sultana raisins, 3 cupfuls citron, 2 cupfuls candied lemon peel, 2 cupfuls almonds, blanched and cut in shreds, ½ pint brandy, 2 ounces each nutmeg, mace and cinnamon, tablespoonful each cloves and allspice. Prepare all these ingredients in following manner : place butter and sugar in large bowl, break eggs into quart measure or pitcher; cover small waiter with clean sheet of paper ; on it lay sifted flour, fruit, citron, and lemon peel, cut into shreds, the almonds and spices, with brandy measured at hand ; also get ready large cake tin (fig. XVIII), by papering it inside with white paper and outside and bottom with 4 or 5 thicknesses of coarse wrapping paper, which can be tied on. Having thus prepared everything, and fire banked up to last, with addition from time to time of a shovelful of coal, by which means you will not reduce oven heat, proceed to beat to very light cream the butter and sugar, adding eggs, 2 at a time, beating a little between each addition, until all are used ; then put in contents of waiter all at once, with brandy ; mix very thoroughly and smooth, put into prepared cake tin, smooth over the top, put plenty of paper on to protect it ; bake 8 hours, keeping oven steadily up to clear, moderate heat ; watch carefully and you will produce a cake worthy of the occasion ; remove from oven very carefully, and suffer it to stay on tin until quite cold ; next day ice it with thin coat of *White Icing*, both top and sides ; place in cool oven to dry the icing. Now spread a second coat of icing, which will prevent any crumbs or fruit being mixed up with the icing when you are icing to finish ; now with broad knife proceed, when first coat is dry, to ice sides, then pour icing on center of cake, in quantity sufficient to reach the edges, when stop ; decorate with vase of white, made flowers, etc., to taste.

Wedding Fruit Cake No. 2. — 1 pound flour, 1 pound sugar, 1 pound butter, 2 pounds currants, 1 pound raisins, ½ pound citron, 1 ounce mace, 1 ounce cinnamon, 4 nutmegs, 1 ounce cloves, 8 eggs, wineglassful brandy, ½ ounce Royal Extract *Rose*.

White Mountain Cake. — 1 cupful butter, 3 cupfuls sugar, 1 pint flour, 1½ teaspoonfuls Royal Baking Powder, whites of 6 eggs, 1 cupful milk. 20 drops Royal Extract *Bitter Almonds*. Rub butter and sugar to light, white cream ; add the 6 whites, whipped to dry froth, the flour, sifted with the powder, the milk, and extract ; mix together thoroughly, but carefully, and bake in jelly cake tins in a quick oven 15 minutes ; then arrange in layers with *White Icing* and grated cocoanut mixed, in the proportion of two cupfuls of former to one of latter.

Icings For Cake.

ALMOND ICING. — 3 whites eggs, 1 pound Jordan (sweet) almonds, 3 cupfuls sugar, 10 drops Royal Extract *Rose*. Pound to fine paste almonds, with a little sugar ; then add whites of eggs, rest of sugar, and extract ; pound few minutes to thoroughly mix. Take up in bowl and use as directed.

Chocolate Transparent Icing. — Melt 3 oz. fine chocolate with small quantity water in pan over fire (stirring constantly) until it becomes soft. Dilute this with ½ a gill of syrup ; work until perfectly smooth. Then add to boiled sugar as above.

Clear Icing, For Cake. -- Put 1 cupful sugar in a bowl, with a tablespoonful lemon juice and whites of 2 eggs. Mix together smooth and pour over the cake ; if the cake is not hot enough to dry it, place it in the mouth of a moderately warm oven.

Transparent Icing. -- Place 1 pound pulverized white sugar in basin with ½ pint water. Boil to consistency of mucilage, then rub sugar with wooden spatula against sides of pan, until it assumes white milky appearance. Stir in two tablespoonfuls Royal Extract Vanilla ; mix well together. Pour this while hot over top of cake, so as to completely cover it.

White Icing. -- The whites of 4 eggs, 1½ pounds white sugar dust, ½ teaspoonful acetic acid (or the juice of half a lemon, ¼ oz. Royal Extract Rose. Place the whites with the sugar in a bowl with the acid and extract. Beat with a wooden spoon until, letting some run from the spoon, it maintains the thread-like appearance for several minutes, when use as directed.

Cheese Cakes.

CHEESE CAKES (Cocoanut.-- Paste, No. 5 ; 1 cupful cocoanut, 1 cupful milk curd, 1 cupful cream, 5 yelks eggs, 1 cupful sugar, 1 teaspoonful Royal Extract Rose. Place cream, curd, eggs, sugar and cocoanut on fire in thick saucepan, when thick, remove, add extract when quite cold ; use it to fill paté pans, lined with the paste, bake in steady oven 10 minutes.

Cheese Cakes (Regent). -- Paste, No. 5 ; 1 quart milk, ½ pint white wine, yelks 6 eggs, 1 cup sugar, ½ cup almonds, blanched and pounded to paste, ½ cupful butter, 1 teaspoonful Royal Extract Orange, 2 tablespoonfuls brandy. Boil milk, then add wine ; suffer to stand until it curds, then strain through fine sieve ; add to curds butter, melted, cream, almonds, paste, extract and brandy ; mix smoothly, use to fill paté pans, lined with the paste ; bake in moderate oven 10 minutes.

Cheese Cakes. -- Pie Paste, No. 3 ; 2 cupfuls milk curd, 1 teaspoonful Royal Extract Nutmeg, ½ cupful cream, yelks two eggs, tablespoonful of brandy, 1 cupful sugar. Put 2 quarts clabbered milk to drain in fine sieve ; when it measures two cupfuls, add to it sugar, brandy, egg yelks, extract, and cream ; mix smooth, and use it to fill paté pans, lined with the paste ; bake in quick oven 10 minutes.

Cheese Cakes (Lemon). -- Paste, No. 3 ; 1 tablespoonful butter, 3½ cupful milk curd, yelks 3 eggs, 1 cupful cream, ½ cupful sugar, 1 teaspoonful Royal Extract Lemon. Place on fire in small stewpan, with butter, sugar, curd, and cream ; stir until little warm, add eggs, soon as thick remove, when cold add extract ; use it to fill paté pans, lined with the paste ; bake in hot oven 8 minutes.

Short Cakes.

PEACH SHORT CAKE. -- 1 quart flour, 1 teaspoonful salt, 2 heaping teaspoonfuls Royal Baking Powder, 2 tablespoonfuls Butter, 1 pint milk. Sift the flour, salt and powder together, rub in the butter cold ; add the milk, and mix into a smooth dough, just soft enough to handle ; divide in half, and roll out to the size of breakfast plates ; lay on a greased baking tin (fig. XIV), and bake in hot oven 20 minutes , separate the cakes without cutting, as cutting makes them heavy. Have two dozen peaches peeled and cut in slices ; use half of them to cover the bottom halves of short cake ; sprinkle plentifully with sugar and cream ; lay on the top halves with the crust downwards ; use the rest of the fruit over them, and sugar plentifully.

Strawberry Short Cake. -- Proceed as directed for Peach Short Cake, substituting strawberries for peaches.

Blackberry Short Cake. -- Proceed as directed for Peach Short Cake, substituting blackberries for peaches.

Raspberry Short Cake. -- Proceed as directed for Peach Short Cake, substituting raspberries for peaches.

Huckleberry Short Cake. -- Proceed as directed for Peach Short Cake, substituting huckleberries for peaches.

Dumplings.

APPLE DUMPLINGS, No. 1. -- Paste, No. 2 ; 6 apples, peeled, cored, and sliced, 1 cupful sugar. Line 6 cups, well greased, with the paste rolled out thin, wet edges, fill with apples, some of the sugar, cover with more paste, put in shallow stewpan, large enough to contain them, with boiling water to reach half-way up the cups ; steam thus 45 minutes ; turn out on dish, sift sugar over them ; serve with Spice Sauce.

Apple Dumplings, No. 2. -- Paste, No. 3 ; 8 apples, peeled and cored, 1 cupful sugar. Roll out the paste thin, cut into 8 squares of 4 inches, lay on each an apple with sugar in aperture made by removing core, wet four corners of paste, and bring them to top of apple and fasten, sift sugar over them, lay on baking sheet and bake in hot oven 25 minutes ; serve with Hard Sauce.

Common Batter. -- 1 cupful flour, ½ teaspoonful Royal Baking Powder, pinch salt, two eggs, 1 cupful milk, 1 tablespoonful sweet oil. Sift flour, salt and powder together, add the oil, eggs beaten and milk ; mix into batter as for griddle cakes, use as directed.

Farina Dumplings. -- 1 quart milk, 10 ounces farina, 3 eggs, 1½ teaspoonfuls of Royal Baking Powder, a tablespoonful of fresh butter, ½ pound fine flour. Bring milk to a boil, stir in farina and boil till well done, continually stirring. After cooled, stir in the melted butter and eggs previously beaten up, and last add sifted flour with baking powder and salt. Drop with tablespoon into boiling water, well salted ; boil about 15 minutes till they rise ; take out with skimmer and serve with fruit sauce.

Liver Dumplings. -- A calf's liver well washed, well skinned and scraped with a sharp knife, taking out all stringy parts ; add to this same quantity of stale wheat bread, grated fine, pepper and salt to taste, some fine cut onions stewed in a little butter may be added if liked ; mix well, form into balls, put into boiling water, well salted, and boil for about 15 minutes ; take out with a skimmer and serve with potatoes and sauce piquante.

Potato Dumplings. -- 1 dozen large potatoes, 6 tablespoonfuls flour, 2 tablespoonfuls Royal Baking Powder, 1 tablespoonful butter, 3 eggs, salt and nutmeg. Grate potatoes, which have been boiled and skinned the day before ; mix with the flour, previously sifted together with baking powder, add the melted butter and eggs one by one, and salt and nutmeg to taste ; form into balls about size of a small apple, put into boiling water, which has been well salted, boil 15 minutes ; take out with skimmer, and serve with any kind of fricassee or pot roast.

Suet Dumplings (Danish). -- 1 cupful suet, chopped fine, 1 cupful grated English muffins or bread, 1 cupful flour, ½ teaspoonful Royal Baking Powder, ½ cupful sugar, 2 eggs, 1 pint milk, large pinch salt. Sift together powder and flour, add beaten eggs, grated muffins, sugar, suet, and milk, form into smooth batter which drop by tablespoonfuls into pint boiling milk, three or four at a time ; when done, dish, and pour over them milk they were boiled in.

THE ROYAL BAKING POWDER IS ABSOLUTELY PURE.

Huckleberry Dumplings.—Proceed as directed for *Apple Dumplings* No. 1.

Peach Dumplings.—Proceed as directed for *Apple Dumplings* No. 1.

Strawberry Dumplings.—Proceed as directed for *Apple Dumplings* No. 1.

Puddings.

COCOANUT PUDDING. ½ pound sugar, ¼ pound butter, ½ pound grated cocoanut, whites of three eggs, 1 teaspoonful Royal Extract *Rose*, 2 tablespoonfuls sherry wine. Beat sugar and butter to a cream ; beat whites until stiff and add to butter and sugar. Add cocoanut last. Bake, and serve with sauce.

Apple Pudding (English).—*Paste*, No. 2 ; 12 or 14 apples, peeled, cored and sliced ; 1 teaspoonful Royal Extract *Nutmeg*, 1½ cupfuls sugar. Line earthenware pudding mould with paste, pack in apples, sugar, and extract ; wet edges ; cover, pinch edges together firmly ; place in saucepan ½ full boiling water.

Apple Pudding (Boston).—*Paste*, No. 3 ; 12 or 14 apples, peeled, cored and sliced ; 1 teaspoonful Royal Extract *Nutmeg*, 1½ cupfuls sugar. Line edge of deep earthenware dish with the paste ; pack in the apples, add sugar, ⅓ cupful water, and extract ; wet edge of paste ; lay on cover of paste ; press two together, ornament the edge, wash with milk, bake in moderate oven ; serve with rich cream.

Apple Tapioca Pudding.—Pare and core enough apples to fill dish ; put into each apple bit of lemon peel. Soak ½ pint tapioca in 1 quart lukewarm water 1 hour, add a little salt ; flavor with lemon ; pour over apples. Bake until apples are tender. Eat when cold, with cream and sugar.

Almond Pudding.—2 *Royal Egg Muffins*, 1 cupful almonds blanched—by pouring boiling water on them till skins slip off easily—and pounded to fine paste, 1½ cupfuls sugar, 4 eggs, 1½ pints milk, 1 teaspoonful each Royal Extract *Bitter Almonds* and *Rose*. Cut off top crust from muffins very thin ; steep them in milk ; beat yelks of eggs and sugar with almonds, then add steeped muffins squeezed a little dry ; dilute with milk, add extract ; put it thus prepared into well buttered earthenware dish ; then stir in gently whites beaten to dry froth ; bake in moderately quick oven about ½ hour.

Arrowroot Pudding.—1 quart milk, 3½ tablespoonfuls arrowroot, 4 eggs, 1 cupful sugar, 1 teaspoonful each Royal Extract *Nutmeg* and *Cinnamon*. Boil milk, add arrowroot dissolved in little water, and the sugar ; let reboil ; take from fire, beat in eggs, whipped a little, and extracts ; pour in well buttered earthenware dish, bake in quick oven ½ an hour ; a few minutes before taking from oven, sift 2 tablespoonfuls sugar over it, and set back to glaze. This pudding is generally eaten cold.

Blackberry Pudding No. 1.—*Paste*, No. 2 ; 1 quart berries, 1½ cupfuls sugar. Proceed as directed for *Apple Pudding*.

Blackberry Pudding No. 2.—Proceed as directed for *Cottage Pudding*, adding 1½ cupfuls blackberries ; serve with *Spice Sauce*.

Bread Pudding No. 1.—3 *Lunch Rolls*, 1 pint milk, ½ pint cream, ½ cupful sugar, 1 tablespoonful butter, 5 eggs, ½ cupful currants, 1 tablespoonful chopped orange peel. Cut off very thin tops and bottoms of rolls ; steep them in milk ; when soaked, place in bowl, after squeezing dry, and milk and cream on fire to boil ; beat eggs, sugar, currants, washed and picked, and orange peel well together ; when milk boils, pour on them, stirring the while. Put in well buttered pudding dish ; bake in steady oven 40 minutes. Serve with *Duchesse Sauce*.

Bread Pudding No. 2.—3 stale *Rolls* or *Muffins*, 3 eggs, 1½ pints milk, 1 cupful sugar, 1 teaspoonful Royal Extract *Lemon*. Steep muffins in milk ; when soaked thoroughly squeeze a little dry, put in bowl with milk to boil ; beat with soaked muffins, sugar, eggs, and extract ; when milk boils, pour on muffins, etc., stir smooth, pour into buttered pudding dish, and bake ¾ hour in moderate, steady oven ; serve with *Hard Sauce* (see *Sauces*).

Bread Pudding No. 3.—3 stale *Sugar Muffins*, 1 pint milk, 5 eggs, 1 tablespoonful butter, pinch salt, 1 cupful seedless raisins, ½ cupful chopped citron, 1 cupful sugar, 1 glass brandy, 1 teaspoonful Royal Extract *Bitter Almonds*. Grate muffins fine ; pour on them, in bowl, the milk, boiling ; cover with plate for ½ hour ; then beat in eggs, sugar, half the raisins, brandy, and extract ; pour it in plain oval mould, well buttered and decorated, with the raisins left out ; set it in saucepan, with boiling water to reach two-thirds up sides of mould ; steam thus 1 hour ; turn out, and serve with *Sugar Sauce*.

Bread and Butter Pudding.—4 *Vienna Rolls* or *Bread*, sliced and buttered, ½ cupful currants, 1½ pints milk, 4 eggs, 1 cupful sugar, 1 teaspoonful Royal Extract *Nutmeg*. Beat eggs and sugar together, add milk and extract ; pour over slices of rolls laid in buttered pudding dish, with currants sprinkled between ; bake ½ hour in quick oven ; serve with *Brandy Sauce*.

Batter Pudding (with Fruit).—1 cupful flour, 1 teaspoonful Royal Baking Powder, pint milk, 4 eggs, 2 cupfuls of any kind fruit prepared as usual, 1½ cupfuls sugar. Sift flour, sugar, and powder together, add eggs, beaten, milk, and fruit, pour into well buttered pudding dish, bake in quick oven 40 minutes ; serve with *Wine Sauce*.

Batter Pudding (Boiled).—1½ cupfuls flour, 1 teaspoonful Royal Baking Powder, ½ teaspoonful salt, 1 tablespoonful butter, 10 drops Royal Extract *Nutmeg*, 2 eggs, 1 pint milk. Sift flour, salt, and powder together ; rub in butter cold ; add eggs, beaten, and milk ; mix into batter as for muffins ; pour into well buttered mould ; set in saucepan, with boiling water two-thirds up sides of mould ; steam 1 hour, and serve with *Spice Sauce*.

Batter Pudding (Baked).—Proceed as directed for *Batter Pudding (boiled)*, baking it in well buttered pudding dish 35 minutes ; serve with *Rexford Sauce*.

Boiled Indian Pudding.—2 cups of Indian meal, 1 pint of milk, 1 cup of flour, ⅛ cup of suet, ½ gill of molasses, 2 cups of dried apples, salt to taste. Boil the milk and pour it scalding on the meal, add the flour, chop the suet fine, soak the apples in a little warm water to swell them, and mix them in the molasses ; add the other ingredients, tie in a pudding cloth, allowing room to swell one-third ; boil or steam 5 hours.

Boston Baked Plum Pudding.—1½ cupfuls beef suet, freed of skin, chopped very fine, 1½ cupfuls raisins, stoned, 1½ cupfuls currants, washed and picked, 1 cupful brown sugar, 2 cupfuls flour, 1 teaspoonful Royal Baking Powder, 4 eggs, 1 cupful milk, ½ cupful citron, chopped, pinch salt, 1 tablespoonful Royal Extract *Nutmeg*, 1 glass brandy. Put all these ingredients in a bowl, eggs as they drop from the shell, flour sifted with powder, and brandy ; mix into rather short batter ; pour into well buttered, clean cake tin, bake in steady oven 2 hours ; serve with *Vanilla Sauce*.

Cottage Pudding.—1 cupful sugar, 2 eggs, 2 cupfuls cream, 1 pint flour, 1½ teaspoonfuls Royal Baking Powder. Beat the eggs and sugar together ; add cream, flour, with the powder sifted in, and pinch salt ; mix into smooth batter as for cup cake ; put into long narrow or oval, buttered mould, bake in hot oven 30 minutes ; serve with *Sauce Aux Quatre Fruits.*

Corn Starch Pudding.—Proceed as directed for *Arrowroot Pudding.*

Cabinet Pudding No. 1. 4 *English muffins or Rolls*, ½ pint milk, 1 pint cream, 4 eggs, and 4 yelks. 1 cupful sugar, ½ cupful almonds, blanched — by pouring boiling water on them until skins slip off easily and cut into shreds, 1 cupful each dried cherries, apricots, greengages, or any other preserved, whole, or canned fruits. Well butter a mould; make layer of muffins cut very thin, then of fruit, almonds, and so on, until all the ingredients are used; beat milk, cream, sugar and eggs together, pour over contents of mould, and let stand before baking at least ½ an hour, then set in saucepan with boiling water to reach two-thirds up mould; steam thus 1 hour; turn out on dish carefully, and serve with *Cream Sauce*.

Cabinet Pudding No. 2. — ½ pound stale sponge cake, ½ cupful raisins, ½ canned peaches, 4 eggs, 1½ pints milk. Butter plain oval mould; lay in some stale cake, third of the raisins stoned, ¼ of peaches; make 2 layers of remainder of cake, raisins, and peaches; cover with very thin slice of bread; then pour over milk beaten with eggs and sugar; set in saucepan with boiling water to reach two-thirds up sides of mould, steam it ¾ hour, turn out carefully on dish, and serve with *Peach Sauce*.

College Pudding. — 3 stale *Royal Egg Muffins* or *Bread*, ½ cupful currants, ½ cupful each chopped citron, orange, and lemon peel, ½ cupful sugar, 3 eggs, 1 pint milk, 1 tablespoonful butter. Grate muffins, place in bowl, pour over milk, boiling; cover with plate 20 minutes, then add beaten eggs, sugar, citron, orange, and lemon peels, melted butter, and currants well washed and picked; mix and fill 6 well greased cups, bake in quick oven 25 minutes; when about to serve, turn out on platter, pour round it *Wine Sauce No. 2*, and serve.

Cracker and Jam Pudding. — 3 eggs, ½ cup cracker crumbs, ½ cup sugar, 1 tablespoonful butter, 1 cup milk, ½ lemon — juice and grated peel, 3 tablespoonfuls of jam. Heat milk and crumbs together until scalding. Turn out to cool, while you rub butter and sugar to a cream, adding the lemon. Stir in beaten yelks, soaked cracker and milk, at last the whites. Butter bake-dish, put jam at the bottom, fill up with the mixture and bake, covered, ½ hour, then brown. Eat cold, with sifted sugar on top, or, if you like, put a meringue over it before taking from oven.

Cottage Pudding. — 1 cup of sugar, 1 cup of milk, 1 egg, lump butter size of egg, 1 pint of flour, salt, 2 heaping teaspoonfuls Royal Baking Powder. SAUCE. — 1 cup sugar, 1 egg, 1 teaspoonful flour, small piece of butter mixed. Add boiling water, let come to boil, flavor with Royal Extract *Vanilla*.

Custard Pudding. — 1½ pints milk, 4 eggs, 1 cupful sugar, 2 teaspoonfuls Royal Extract *Vanilla*. Beat eggs and sugar together; dilute with milk, and extract; pour into buttered pudding dish, set in oven in dripping pan, two-thirds full of boiling water; bake until firm, about 40 minutes in moderate oven.

Chocolate Pudding. — 1 quart of milk scalded; 1½ squares of chocolate, grated; wet with cold milk, and stir into scalded milk. When chocolate is dissolved, pour into pudding dish; add yelks of 6 eggs, well beaten, and 6 tablespoonfuls of sugar. Bake about ¾ of an hour. Beat whites of eggs to stiff froth; add 6 tablespoonfuls sugar. Spread the frosting over top; set again in oven until a light brown.

Charlotte Russe. — 1 pint of cream, kept on ice 5 or 6 hours until perfectly cool, beat until stiff. Then take a large teaspoonful of gelatine, dissolve over the fire in a little milk. When cold mix with cream. Add ½ pound of powdered sugar, 2 teaspoonfuls of Royal Extract *Vanilla*. Put in moulds lined with sponge cake and set on ice till perfectly cold.

Farina Pudding. — Proceed as directed for *Arrowroot Pudding*.

Fig Pudding. — ½ pound good dried figs, washed, wiped and minced; 2 cups fine dry bread crumbs, 3 eggs, ½ cup beef suet, powdered; 2 scant cups of sweet milk, ½ cup white sugar, little salt, ½ teaspoonful Royal Baking Powder, dissolved in hot water and stirred into milk. Soak the crumbs in milk, add eggs, beaten light with sugar, salt, suet and figs. Beat 3 minutes, put in buttered mould with tight top set in boiling water with weight on cover to prevent mould from upsetting, and boil 3 hours. Eat hot with hard sauce or butter, powdered sugar, 1 teaspoonful Royal extract *Nutmeg*.

German Pudding. — 3 large potatoes, pinch salt, 1 cupful suet chopped, ½ cupful coffee sugar, 1 egg, ½ teaspoonful Royal Baking Powder, 1 tablespoonful flour, ¼ cupful cream. Peel, boil, and mash potatoes very fine; add egg, cream, sugar, and salt; when cold add suet and flour sifted with powder; bake in buttered pudding dish 30 minutes, in rather quick oven; serve with *Wine Sauce No. 1*.

Hominy Pudding. — ⅔ cupful hominy, 1½ pints milk, 2 eggs, 1 tablespoonful butter, 1 teaspoonful Royal Extract *Rose*, 1 cupful sugar. Boil hominy in milk 1 hour; then pour it on eggs, extract, and sugar, beaten together; add butter, pour in buttered pudding dish, bake in hot oven 20 minutes.

Huckleberry Pudding. — 3 stale *Sugar Muffins* or *bread*, 3 cupfuls huckleberries, 1 cupful sugar, 1 teaspoonful each Royal Extract *Cinnamon* and *Cloves*, 1½ pints milk, 3 eggs, pinch salt. Grate muffins, place in bowl, pour over milk, boiling, cover with plate, stand 30 minutes; add eggs, beaten, sugar, salt, extract, and berries; mix and put into buttered pudding dish, and bake in moderate oven 45 minutes; serve with *Spice Sauce*.

Indian Pudding No. 1. — 3 *Corn Muffins* or *Bread*, 1½ pints milk, ½ cupful sugar, 3 eggs, 1 teaspoonful each Royal Extract *Ginger* and *Cinnamon*, 1 pinch salt. Steep muffins in milk; when soaked, squeeze rather dry, place in bowl, beat up with sugar, salt, eggs, and extracts, pour milk over them, boiling, stirring all the while, pour in buttered pudding dish, and bake 1 hour in moderate oven; serve with *Hard Sauce*.

Indian Pudding No. 2. — ½ cupful flour, 1½ cupfuls corn meal, ½ cupful syrup, ½ teaspoonful salt, 1 quart milk. Mix flour, corn meal, salt and cupful of milk together, pour the rest on it, boiling, stir once in a while for 30 minutes; bake in moderate oven 2 hours, in well buttered pudding dish; serve with *Wine Sauce*.

Lemon Pudding. — 2 stale *Sally Lunn Muffins* or *Bread*, juice 2 lemons, 1 teaspoonful Royal Extract *Lemon*, 1 cupful sugar, 4 eggs, 1 tablespoonful butter, 1 pint milk. Grate muffins, put in bowl, pour in milk, boiling, cover with plate, set aside for 30 minutes, then add sugar, butter, beaten eggs, extract, and juice; mix together, and pour into well buttered pudding dish; bake in rather hot oven 45 minutes; serve with *Lemon sauce*.

Lemon Suet Pudding. — 4 *English Muffins* or stale *Bread*, 1 cupful suet, ½ cupful sugar, 4 eggs, 1 tablespoonful Royal Extract *Lemon*, 1½ pints milk, pinch salt. Grate muffins, chop suet, freed of skin, very fine, put them in bowl, add sugar, eggs, beaten, salt and extract, pour over boiling milk, stirring it the while, suffer it to stand 30 minutes covered; then pour into well buttered pudding dish, bake in moderate oven 40 minutes; serve with *Sugar Sauce*.

Macaroni Pudding. — 1 cupful broken Italian macaroni, 1½ pints milk, 4 eggs, 1 cupful sugar, 1 large tablespoonful butter, 1 teaspoonful Royal Extract *Vanilla*. Boil macaroni in well salted water 10 minutes, then add to the boiling milk and simmer 20 minutes longer; remove from fire, pour on sugar, eggs, and butter beaten together, lastly add extract; put in well buttered pudding dish, bake in steady oven 35 minutes; serve with *Cream Sauce*.

THE ROYAL BAKING POWDER IS ABSOLUTELY PURE.

Meringue Rice Pudding.—Take teacupful rice to 1 pint water: when rice is boiled dry add 1 pint milk, a piece butter size of an egg, and 5 eggs. Beat yelks and grated rind of lemon, and mix with rice. Butter dish, pour in mixture, bake lightly. Beat whites to stiff froth; add cup of sugar and juice of a lemon. When pudding is nearly done, spread on frosting, bake in slow oven till top is light brown.

Orange Pudding.—1½ cupfuls stale *Royal Unfermented Bread*, 1 cupful finely chopped suet, 1 cupful sugar, 2 eggs, juice of 1 orange, 1 tablespoonful Royal Extract *Orange*, ½ cupful milk. Mix all thoroughly together, fill 6 cups well greased, boil 30 minutes. Turn out on dish, serve with *Hard Sauce*, flavored with 1 teaspoonful Royal Extract *Orange*.

Plum Pudding, No. 1 (Royal Christmas).—2 cupfuls raisins, 2 cupfuls currants, 2 cupfuls suet, ½ cupful almonds, blanched, 2 cupfuls flour, 2 cupfuls grated *Royal Sugar Muffins* or *Bread*, ½ cupful each, citron, orange, and lemon peel, 8 eggs, 1 cupful sugar, ½ cupful cream, 1 gill each wine and brandy, large pinch salt, 1 tablespoonful Royal Extract *Nutmeg*, 1 teaspoonful Royal Baking Powder. Put in large bowl raisins, seeded, currants, washed and picked, suet, chopped very fine, almonds cut fine, citron, orange, and lemon peels, chopped, lemon, sugar, wine, brandy, and cream, lastly; add flour, sifted with powder, mix all well together; put in large, well buttered mould (fig. II); set in saucepan with boiling water to reach half up sides of mould, steam thus five hours; turn out on dish carefully; serve with *Royal Wine Sauce*.

Plum Pudding No. 2.—1½ cupfuls each grated *Lunch Rolls* or *Bread*, very finely chopped suet, raisins, seeded, currants, washed and picked, and coffee sugar, ½ cupful each citron, milk and orange marmalade, 4 eggs, two cupfuls flour, 1 teaspoonful Royal Baking Powder, 1 teaspoonful each Royal Extract *Cinnamon*, *Cloves*, and *Nutmeg*. Mix all these ingredients well together in large bowl, put in well buttered mould; set in saucepan with boiling water to reach half up its sides; steam thus 3½ hours; turn out carefully on dish, and serve with *Royal Wine Sauce*.

Plum Pudding No. 3.—1½ cupfuls finely chopped suet, 2 cupfuls raisins, seeded, 1 cupful currants, washed and picked, ½ cupful coffee sugar, ½ cupful chopped citron, 1 glass white wine, 2½ cupfuls flour, 1 teaspoonful Royal Baking Powder, 1 cupful milk, 1 teaspoonful each Royal Extract *Nutmeg* and *Lemon*. Place all these ingredients in bowl, with eggs beaten, and flour, sifted with powder, mix into firm batter; put in well buttered mould, set in saucepan with boiling water to reach half up its sides; steam thus 2½ hours; turn out carefully on dish; serve with *Hard Sauce*.

Plum Pudding No. 4 (English Christmas).—2 cupfuls each stoned raisins, currants, washed and picked, beef suet, chopped fine, and coffee sugar, 3 cupfuls grated *English Muffins* or *Bread*, 8 eggs, 1 cupful each chopped citron, and almonds blanched—by pouring hot water on them until the skins slip off easily—1 lemon peel, and large pinch salt. Mix all these ingredients in large bowl, put in well buttered mould, set in saucepan with boiling water to reach two-thirds up its sides, steam thus 5 hours, turn out carefully on dish, serve with brandy poured over it, and *Brandy Sauce* in bowl. When about to serve on table, brandy should be set on fire.

"Poor Man's Pudding."—½ cupful suet, chopped, ½ cupful seeded raisins, ½ cupful currants, washed and picked, 1½ cupfuls grated *Corn Muffins* or *Bread*, 1 cupful flour, 1 teaspoonful Royal Baking Powder, ½ cupful brown sugar, 1 pint milk. Mix all well together, put into well greased mould, set in saucepan with boiling water to reach half up sides of mould; steam two hours; turn out on dish, carefully; serve with butter and sugar.

Plum Pudding (French).—½ pound beef kidney suet, ½ pound raisins (Smyrna and Malaga mixed), ½ pound fresh bread crumbs, 1 tablespoonful flour, 6 ounces brown sugar, 4 ounces orange peel and citron mixed, a little salt, ¼ of a grated nutmeg, a pinch of pulverized ginger and a little lemon peel chopped fine, about 5 eggs, about 2 tablespoonfuls good brandy or rum, and ½ tablespoonful sweet cream. This is sufficient for a good-sized pudding. Wash the raisins in lukewarm water, place them in basin or wooden bowl, with the peel already cut into square pieces, and steep in a little brandy. Now trim the beef kidney fat and chop it very fine, with one spoonful flour, mix it well with the crumbs of bread, brown sugar and the eggs; then add the raisins, the peel, the rest of the brandy, salt, nutmeg, ginger, and, last of all, and after it is all well mixed, the cream. Spread all this in a large napkin, well buttered, fold up the corners of the napkin, and tie to the level of the pudding, so as to make it round; then plunge the pudding into a saucepan of boiling water, and let it boil at least 4 hours—constant boiling. Take out and let drain in a sieve; cut it from the top so as to keep on a level, then turn it out on a dish, removing the napkin carefully, so as not to disturb the fine part of the pudding. Sprinkle with a little rum sauce. You may apply a match to the pudding when it is on the table. Serve a little rum sauce separate. This pudding may be cooked in a mould, the mould well buttered, and the pudding tied in a napkin, also well buttered. Boil 4 hours.

Princess Pudding.—⅜ cupful butter, 1 cupful sugar, 1 large cupful flour, 3 eggs, ½ teaspoonful Royal Baking Powder, small glass brandy. Rub to smooth cream butter and sugar, add eggs, 1 at a time, beating few minutes between, add flour, sifted with powder, and brandy; put into mould, well buttered, set in saucepan with boiling water to reach half up its sides; steam thus 1½ hours; turn out on dish carefully; serve with *Lemon Sauce*.

Rice Pudding No. 1.—½ cupful rice, 1½ pints milk, ½ cupful sugar, large pinch salt, 1 tablespoonful lemon rind chopped fine. Put rice, washed and picked, sugar, salt, and milk in quart pudding dish; bake in moderate oven 2 hours, stirring frequently first 1¼ hours, then permit it to finish cooking, with light colored crust, disturbing it no more. Eat cold, with cream.

Rice Pudding No. 2.—1 cupful rice, 1 quart milk, 4 eggs, 1 tablespoonful butter, 1 cupful sugar, pinch salt. Boil rice in 1 pint milk until tender, then remove from fire; add eggs, sugar, salt, and milk, beaten together, mix; pour in pudding dish, break butter in small pieces on surface; bake in steady oven 30 minutes; serve with *Brandy Sauce*.

Rice Pudding No. 3.—½ cupful rice, ¾ pint milk, 4 apples, peeled, cored, and stewed, ⅓ cupful sugar, 4 eggs. Boil rice in milk until reduced to pulp, beat well with apple sauce and sugar for 10 minutes, then set aside to cool, then carefully mix in whites of eggs, whipped to stiff froth, butter the mould, pour in pudding, set in saucepan with boiling water to reach half up its sides; steam slowly for 25 minutes; permit it to stand 3 minutes before turning out; serve with *Custard Sauce*.

Sago Pudding.—1 quart milk, 4 tablespoonfuls sago boiled in the milk till soft; set dish in kettle of hot water, and let sago swell gradually. Beat up 3 eggs, and stir into cooked milk and sago; salt and sugar to taste. Then put in oven and bake very lightly. Sauce for this: ¾ cupful butter beaten to cream, stir in sugar till quite thick. To cupful boiling water, add corn starch mixed with cold water, till the whole is of consistency of thin starch: mix this with sugar and butter, pour ½ over pudding while warm, and other half just before serving, after adding 1 teaspoonful Royal Extract *Vanilla*, *Lemon* or *Nutmeg* to give a rich flavor.

Souffle of Different Fruits. — With fruits of a soft and juicy nature, such as peaches, plums, apricots, bananas, etc., proceed in this manner: Remove the kernels and press the fruit through a sieve; put what you have thus obtained in a bowl, adding ½ pound of powdered sugar and the whites of three eggs; beat well with an egg-beater for 5 or 6 minutes. Then take the whites of 6 or 7 eggs and beat them into a stiff froth; mix well together. Put this on a dish in a well-heated oven 5 or 6 minutes before serving. Sprinkle powdered sugar on top. For hard fruits, such as apples, pears, etc., cook them first and then press through a sieve. The treatment is exactly the same as for the others.

Sweet Potato Pudding. — Six good sized potatoes, grated raw; 1 tablespoonful of butter, 1 tablespoonful of lard, 1 pint molasses, 3 tablespoonfuls brown sugar, ½ pint milk, 1 egg, 1 teaspoonful each cloves, allspice and ginger, 2 teaspoonfuls salt; water to make a soft batter; stir two or three times while baking; bake slowly for 2 hours.

Tapioca Pudding. — 1 cupful tapioca, soaked in 1 quart cold water over night, 1 cupful sugar, 1½ pints milk. 4 eggs. Proceed as directed for *Rice Pudding* No. 2.

Tapioca Pudding. — 1 small cupful tapioca, 1 quart milk, 1 teaspoonful butter, 3 tablespoonfuls sugar. Soak tapioca in water 4 or 5 hours, then add the milk; flavor with Royal Extract *Lemon*, or anything else you prefer. Bake slowly 1 hour. To be made day before it is wanted, and eaten cold with cream or milk and sugar. Some prefer the pudding made with 3 pints milk and no water.

Tapioca and Cocoanut Pudding. — 1 cup tapioca, soaked over night, 1 quart milk, yelks 4 eggs, whites of 2, 1 cupful sugar, 2 tablespoonfuls grated cocoanut; bake ½ hour. Make frosting of whites 2 eggs, 3 tablespoonfuls sugar, 2 tablespoonfuls grated cocoanut; spread over pudding when baked. Set in oven until a light brown.

Vermicelli Pudding. — Proceed as directed for *Macaroni Pudding.*

Pies.

PASTE FOR PIES, No. 1. — 3 cupfuls *sifted* flour, ½ teaspoonful Royal Baking Powder, large pinch salt, 1 cupful cream, ½ cupful butter. Sift flour, salt, and powder together; add the cream; mix into smooth, rather firm paste; flour the board, roll it out thin; spread the butter on it evenly, fold in three; roll out thin, and fold in three; repeat twice more, and use.

Paste No. 2. — 3 cupfuls flour, ½ teaspoonful Royal Baking Powder, ½ pound beef suet, freed of skin, and chopped very fine, 1 cupful water. Place the flour, sifted with the powder, in bowl, add suet and water; mix into smooth, rather firm dough.

Paste No. 3. — 3 cupfuls *sifted* flour, ½ cupful lard, 1½ cupfuls butter, ½ teaspoonful Royal Baking Powder, 1 cupful water. Cut lard into flour, sifted with powder; mix into smooth, firm paste with the water; place it to cool for 15 minutes; meanwhile, press milk and salt from butter, by pressing in clean, wet towel, and flour it. Roll out dough on well floured board, place butter on it, fold dough over it, completely covering butter; roll it out, lightly, to ½ inch in thickness, turn it over, fold each end to middle, flour it, roll out again; fold ends to middle, and turn it; repeat this 3 times more, and use. If this paste is made in summer, put on ice between each operation of folding and rolling.

Paste No. 4. — 5 cupfuls flour, 1 cupful butter, 1 cupful lard, 1 cupful water, ½ teaspoonful Royal Baking Powder. Sift flour with powder; rub in lard and butter cold; add the water, mix into a smooth lithe dough.

Puff Paste No. 5. — 3 cupfuls *sifted* flour, 2 cupfuls butter, 1 egg yelk, a little salt, 1 teaspoonful Royal Baking Powder. This is difficult to make. The essentials are: A cool place to make it in, ice, broken up in two shallow cake pans, good flour, and butter, firm, with salt and buttermilk worked out. Sift flour with powder in it on pastry slab, form it in a ring with back of your hand; place in center the egg yelk and salt, add a little ice water, and from inside of ring gradually take flour, adding a little at a time, as you require it, more ice water, about a cupful together, until you have smooth, fine paste, very tenacious and lithe. Place in ice-box 15 minutes, then roll out to size of a dinner plate; lay on it butter, and wrap over it edges of dough, carefully covering it; turn it upside down, roll out very thin; then turn face down — the face is side of the paste next to rolling-pin — folding it in three, squarely; repeat this *three times more*, placing it in thin tin on the broken ice, and other tin containing ice *on it*, between each turn or operation of folding and rolling. By this method this difficult *Puff Paste* may be made successfully in hot-test weather.

Paste No. 6. — 3 cupfuls *sifted* flour, 1 large cupful butter, ½ teaspoonful Royal Baking Powder, 3 tablespoonfuls sugar, ½ cupful milk. Sift flour with powder and sugar, rub in butter, add milk; mix into a smooth dough of medium stiffness.

Paste No. 7 (Timbale Paste). — 3 cupfuls sifted flour, 1¼ cupfuls butter, yelks 2 eggs, ⅔ cup ice water. ½ teaspoonful Royal Baking Powder. Sift together flour and powder on pastry slab, form it in ring with back of the hand; put in middle the butter and egg yelks, which gradually work together; then add water, a little at a time, using the flour from inside of the ring, until the whole is formed into a very smooth paste.

Apple Pie No. 1. — 5 or 6 apples, 1 cupful sugar, ⅓ cup water, 1 teaspoonful Royal Extract *Lemon, Paste No. 4.* Peel, quarter, and core apples, put in stewpan with sugar and water; when tender, remove; when cold, add extract and fill pie plate, lined with the paste; wet the edges, cover with paste rolled out thin, and wash with milk; bake in steady, moderate oven 20 minutes.

Apple Pie No. 2. — 3 tart apples, ½ cupful sugar, ½ lemon rind grated, *Paste No. 4.* Peel, core, and slice apples very thin; line pie plate with paste; put in apples, sugar, and little water; wet the edges with paste rolled out very thin: wash with milk, bake in steady, moderate oven 25 minutes — or till apples are cooked.

Apple Pot Pie. — 14 apples, peeled, cored and sliced, 1½ pints flour, 1 teaspoonful Royal Baking Powder, 1 cupful sugar, ½ cupful butter, 1 cupful milk, large pinch salt. Sift flour with powder and salt, rub in butter cold, add milk, mix into dough as for tea biscuits; with it line shallow stewpan to within two inches of bottom; pour in 1½ cupfuls water, apples, and sugar; wet edges and cover with rest of dough; put cover on, set it to boil 20 minutes, then place in moderate oven until apples are cooked; then remove from oven, cut top crust in four equal parts; dish apples, lay on them pieces of side crust cut in diamonds, and pieces of top crust on a plate; serve with cream.

A Delicate and Rich Desert is of Cream Pie and Oranges. — Cut the oranges in thin slices and sprinkle sugar over them; let them stand for 2 or 3 hours; serve on ordinary fruit plates. The pie is made with a bottom crust only, and that not thick, but light and flaky. Take 1 coffeecupful of thick, sweet cream, ½ cupful of pulverized sugar, 1 tablespoonful flour, 1 egg; flavor with Royal Extract *Lemon*; bake until you are sure the crust is brown and hard, so that it will not absorb the custard.

Blackberry Pie. — *Paste No. 4*, ½ cup sugar, and three cupfuls berries to each pie. Line pie plate with paste, put in berries and sugar, wet the edges, cover and wash with milk; bake in quick, steady oven 20 minutes.

Cocoanut Pie.—Proceed as for *Custard Pie, plain*, adding 1½ cupfuls grated cocoanut, and leaving out ½ pint milk.

Cranberry Pie.—*Paste* No. 4, 3 cups cranberries, stewed with 1½ cupfuls sugar, and strained. Line pie plate with paste; put in cranberry jam, wash the edges, lay 3 narrow bars across; fasten at edge, then 3 more across, forming diamond shaped spaces, lay rim of *Paste* 5, or of same; wash with egg wash, bake in quick oven until paste is cooked.

Custard Pie (Plain).—*Paste* No. 6, 1½ pints milk, 4 eggs, 1 cup sugar, 1 teaspoonful Royal Extract *Lemon*. Line well greased pie plate ¼ inch thick, take ball of paste, flour it well, and proceed with palm of left hand, pressed against edge, to push the paste from center into a thick, high rim on edge of plate. Fill while in oven with sugar, eggs, and milk, beaten with extract, and strained; bake in moderate oven 20 minutes.

Custard Pie (Apple).—Proceed as for *Custard Pie* (*Peach*) substituting thick, stewed apples.

Custard Pie (Peach).—Proceed as for *Custard Pie, plain*, laying in bottom of pie some cooked, fresh, or canned peaches, then adding the custard.

Cherry Pie.—*Paste* No. 3, 3 cupfuls cherries, stemmed, 1 cupful sugar. Line pie plate with the paste, wet edges, add cherries, cover, bake in steady, quick oven 25 minutes.

Currant Pie.—*Paste* No. 3, 3 cupfuls ripe currants, stewed 10 minutes with cupful sugar, and strained. Proceed to make as for *Cranberry Pie*.

Dried Apple Pie.—Stew apples until quite soft, rub through a colander, have them juicy. Beat two eggs, saving the white of one; ½ cup butter, ½ cup sugar to every pie; season to taste. Quantity of sugar must be governed somewhat by the acidity of the apples. Bake with a bottom crust; while they are baking make a frosting of the white of 1 egg; when pies are done spread frosting evenly over the top; set again in the oven and brown slightly.

French Plum Pie.—*Paste* No. 4, 2 cups French prunes steeped in water over night, 1 cup sugar, 1 teaspoonful Royal Extract *Lemon*. Line pie plate with paste; wet edges; add prunes with sugar, ½ cupful water and extract; cover, wash with milk, bake in rather hot oven 25 minutes.

Gooseberry Pie.—*Paste* No. 5, 3 cups gooseberries, stewed with 1½ cupfuls sugar 15 minutes, and strained. Proceed as directed for *Cranberry Pie*.

Lemon Cream Pie.—*Paste* No. 5, 1½ pints milk, 3 tablespoonfuls corn starch, 1 cup sugar, 2 tablespoonfuls butter, 1 teaspoonful each Royal Extract *Lemon*, *Cloves* and *Cinnamon*, juice of 2 lemons, yelks 4 eggs. Boil milk, add corn starch dissolved in a little milk; when it reboils, take off, beat in yelks, butter, lemon juice and extracts; pour at once into pie plates lined with paste, having high rim—as described in *Custard Pie*—bake in hot oven, until paste is cooked, about 20 minutes.

Lemon Cream Meringue Pie.—Having made the *Lemon Cream Pie*, whip 4 whites of eggs to dry froth; gently incorporate 1 cupful sugar; spread over top of pie; return to oven to set fawn color.

Lovers of Chocolate, in any and every form, can make this addition to a common custard pie. Beat 1 egg to a stiff froth, then add pulverized sugar and grated chocolate with ½ teaspoonful Royal Extract *Vanilla*; spread this on the top of the pie and let it harden for a moment in the oven. Or you may prepare it in still another way. Put the chocolate in a basin on the back of the stove, and let it melt (do not put a drop of water with it); when melted beat 1 egg and some sugar in with it; in the latter case it will be a regular chocolate brown in color, and in the other a sort of gray.

Lemon Pie.—*Paste* No. 6, 2 soda crackers, 2 lemons, 1½ cupfuls coffee sugar, 2 eggs, 1½ cupfuls boiling water. Roll crackers fine; place in bowl, pour on boiling water; cover with plate; when cold add eggs, beaten, sugar, grated rind of one, and juice of both lemons. Line pie plate with paste; add preparation; wet edges; cover, wash over with milk, bake in quick oven 25 minutes.

Marlborough Pie.—*Paste* No. 5, 1½ cups stewed apples, 3 eggs, 1 tablespoonful butter, 1 gill cream, 8 macaroons, 2 tablespoonfuls brandy, 2 tablespoonfuls chopped citron. Beat macaroons fine; add apples and eggs, beat 5 minutes; then add melted butter, cream, citron and brandy; mix together well. Line deep pie plate; wash edges; lay thin rim on; wash with egg wash; pour in the preparations, and bake in moderate oven 25 minutes.

Orange Pie.—*Paste* No. 5, 4 eggs, 2 tablespoonfuls butter, ½ pint cream, 1 cup sugar, juice of two oranges and rind of one. Beat butter and sugar to light cream; add beaten eggs gradually with juice and rind, grated; lastly add cream whipped to stiff froth; line pie plate with paste; wash edges; put on rim; pour in mixture, bake in slow oven 25 minutes.

Mince Pie.—*Paste* 3, 2 cupfuls mince meat.

Mince-meat No. 1.—7 lbs. currants, 3½ lbs. peeled and cored apples, 3½ lbs. beef, 3½ lbs. suet, ½ lb. each citron, lemon and orange peel, 2½ lbs. coffee sugar, 2 lbs. raisins, 4 nutmegs, 1 oz. cinnamon, ½ oz. each cloves and mace, 1 pint brandy, and 1 pint white wine. Wash currants, dry, pick them, stone the raisins, remove skin and sinews from beef and suet, chop each ingredient separately, very fine, put into large pan as they are finished, finally adding spices, brandy and wine; thoroughly mix together; pack in jars; store in cold, dry place. This mince-meat will keep from 12 to 18 months. The fruit should never be floured in making mince pie.

Mince-meat No. 2.—2 lbs. currants, 5 lbs. peeled and cored apples, 2 lbs. lean, boiled beef, 1 lb. beef suet, ¾ lb. citron, 2½ lbs. coffee sugar, 2 lbs. raisins, 1 lb. seedless raisins, 2 tablespoonfuls cinnamon, 1 nutmeg, 1 tablespoonful each mace, cloves and allspice, 1 pint each Madeira wine and brandy. Wash currants, dry, pick them, stone the raisins, remove skin and sinews from the beef, chop each ingredient up separately, very fine; place soon as done in large pan, finally adding spices, Madeira and brandy; mix thoroughly; pack in jars; keep in cold place.

Mince-meat No. 3.—2 lbs. currants, 2 lbs. beef suet, 1 lb. raisins, 1¼ lbs. coffee sugar, 4 ozs. candied orange peel, red and white wine each ½ pint, peels of 2 lemons very thin, 1 teaspoonful each cinnamon, cloves and nutmeg; wash currants, stone the raisins, free suet of skin; chop each ingredient separately, very fine; put soon as done in pan, finally adding spices and wines; mix thoroughly; pack in jar; store in cold place. Line pie plate with the paste; wet edges; put in mince-meat; cover, wash over with egg, bake in quick oven 25 minutes.

How to Distribute Raisins in a Mince Pie.—When the mince-meat is ready to be put in the crust, prepare the raisins and put them in a basin on the stove with enough water to cover them. Cook until tender; after you fill the crust you can put raisins in so that about same number will come in each piece. Then, if you wet the edges of the crust so that no juice can escape, you will never know by the taste that the raisins were not cooked with the mince-meat.

Peach Pie.—*Paste* No. 5, 8 peaches peeled and stoned, 1 cup sugar. Line pie plate with the paste; wet edges; arrange peaches; add sugar; lay 3 narrow bars paste across; fasten ends, lay 3 more bars, to form diamond spaces; wet again and lay rim over; wash over with egg; bake in moderate oven 20 minutes.

Plum Pie. — *Paste* No. 5, 3 cupfuls plums; simmer in water, cover with 1½ cupfuls sugar, until tender. Line pie plate with the paste; wet edges; cover, wash with egg, bake in quick oven 20 minutes.

Pumpkin Pie. — Take large sized pumpkin, firm, of deep color, wash and boil just as you would potatoes with skin on; when thoroughly cooked pass carefully through sieve, clearing it of all lumps, seeds, etc. Take 1 cup brown sugar, 1 cup molasses, mix well together. Beat the whites and yelks of 4 eggs well together and mix with the pumpkin thoroughly; then add the molasses and sugar, pinch of salt, 4 teaspoonfuls best ginger, 1 teaspoonful ground cinnamon; take 1 cup milk, mix well altogether. This is intended to make 6 pies; should pumpkin not be a large one, add less milk so as not to get too thin. Bake in deep plate lined with plain pastry. Squash pie made in same way.

Pumpkin Pie No. 1. — *Paste* No. 4, 1 pint stewed pumpkin, 3 eggs, 1½ pints milk, 2 teaspoonfuls ginger, 1 teaspoonful each nutmeg, cloves, cinnamon and mace, pinch salt and 1 cupful light brown sugar. Stew pumpkin as follows: Cut pumpkin, of deep color, firm and close in texture, in half; remove seeds, but do not peel it; cut in small slices, put in shallow stewpan, with about ½ cupful water; cover very tight; soon as steam forms, set where it will not burn; when pumpkin is tender, turn off liquor and set it back on stove to steam dry; then measure out, after straining, 1 pint, add milk boiling, sugar mixed with spices and salt, and well mix altogether; add eggs, beaten, last. Line pie plate in manner described for *Custard Pie, plain*, pour in prepared pumpkin; bake in quick, steady oven about 30 minutes, until pie is firm in center.

Pumpkin Pie No. 2. — *Paste* No. 4, 1 pint pumpkin stewed as for *Pie* No. 1, 1 egg, 2 tablespoonfuls molasses, ¼ pint milk, ½ pint thin cream, ½ cupful sugar, 1 tablespoonful Royal Extract *Ginger*. Place pumpkin in bowl, beat in molasses, sugar, egg, and ginger; then pour in milk and thin cream, boiling. Line tin as described for *Custard Pie, plain*, pour in pumpkin preparation, bake in good hot oven until firm in center - about 30 minutes.

Raspberry Pie. — *Paste* No. 3, 3 cupfuls raspberries, 1 cupful sugar. Line pie plate with the paste, prick over with fork to prevent shrinking and blistering; cut a top crust out a little larger than the other, prick also and bake; put the fruit and sugar in the pie plate, and cover with the top crust; if the fruit is ripe they will steam tender; if not, just return to the oven until hot through.

Rice Pie. — *Paste* No. 4, ½ cup rice, ½ pint milk, ½ pint cream, 3 eggs, pinch salt, 1 cupful sugar. Boil rice in ½ pint water and milk, until very soft; then rub through sieve, add the cream, beaten eggs, salt, and sugar. Line pie plate as directed for *Custard Pie, plain*, pour in rice mixture; bake in hot oven about 25 minutes.

Rhubarb Pie. — *Paste* No. 4, 1½ bunches rhubarb, 1½ cupfuls sugar. Cut fruit in small pieces after stripping off skin, cook it very fast in shallow stewpan, with sugar. Line pie plate with the paste; wet rim; add rhubarb, cold; lay 3 bars paste across, fastening ends; lay 3 more across, forming diamond-shaped spaces; lay round a rim, wash over with egg, and bake in quick oven 15 minutes.

Strawberry Pie. — Proceed as directed for *Raspberry Pie*.

Huckleberry Pie. — *Paste* No. 3, 3 cupfuls huckleberries, 1 cupful sugar. Line pie plate with the paste, wet the edges, add berries, washed and picked over, and sugar; cover, wash with milk, bake in quick oven 20 minutes.

Sauces For Puddings, Etc.

BRANDY SAUCE. — Proceed as directed for *Wine Sauce*, No. 2, substituting brandy for wine.

Currant Jelly Sauce. — Melt 1 cupful red currant jelly, 1 glass white wine, and 1 teaspoonful Royal Extract *Raspberry*.

Cream Sauce. — Bring ¾ pint cream slowly to boil; set in stewpan of boiling water; when it reaches boiling point add sugar, then pour slowly on whipped whites of 2 eggs in bowl; add 1 teaspoonful Royal Extract *Vanilla*, and use.

Custard Sauce. — 1 pint milk, yelks 4 eggs, ½ cupful sugar. Set over fire, and stir until thick.

Duchesse Sauce. — Boil 2 ounces grated chocolate in half pint milk 5 minutes; strain on 2 yelks of eggs beaten with ½ gill cream, and ½ cupful sugar, strain, return to fire, stir until thick as honey; remove, and add 1 teaspoonful Royal Extract *Vanilla*.

German Sauce. — Set on the fire in tin pail, placed in a stewpan half full boiling water, 1 cupful cream and cupful milk; when it reaches boiling point, add sugar and yelks of 4 eggs with small pinch salt; whisk very quickly until it has appearance of thick cream very frothy; just before serving, add tablespoonful very good butter, 1 teaspoonful each Royal Extract *Nutmeg* and *Vanil a*, and 1 wineglass white rum.

Hard Sauce. — Beat one cupful sugar and ½ cupful butter to white cream; add whites 2 eggs, beat few minutes longer; tablespoonful brandy, and teaspoonful Royal Extract *Nutmeg*; put on ice until needed.

Hygienic Cream Sauce. — ½ pint milk, ½ pint cream, yelk 1 egg, 1 tablespoonful buckwheat dissolved in little milk, large pinch salt. Bring milk and cream to boil, in thick, well lined saucepan; add to it buckwheat dissolved in milk, stirring rapidly to prevent lumping, allow it to boil 5 minutes; remove from fire, beat in the yelk of egg diluted with a tablespoonful milk. This is better and far more healthful (especially for children) than so much butter and syrup. Syrup, minus butter, is well enough, but use of butter with hot cakes cannot be recommended.

Lemon Sauce. — Boil 1 cupful sugar and 1 cupful water together 15 minutes, then remove; when cooled a little, add ½ teaspoonful Royal Extract *Lemon* and 1 tablespoonful lemon juice.

Peach Sauce. — Place peach juice from can in small saucepan; add equal volume of water; little more sugar, and 8 or 10 raisins, boil this 10 minutes, strain and just before serving, add 8 drops Royal Extract *Bitter Almonds*.

Maple Syrup. — ½ pound maple sugar, 1 pound cut sugar, 3 pints water. Break maple sugar small, place on fire, with cut sugar and water; boil 5 minutes; skim, then cool.

Rexford Sauce. — Dissolve 1 teaspoonful corn starch in little water, add it to one cupful boiling water, with ⅔ cupful brown sugar; boil 10 minutes; remove from fire; add ½ cupful cider, scalding hot, 1 large tablespoonful good butter, and yelks 2 eggs.

Royal Wine Sauce. — Bring slowly to boiling point ½ pint wine; then add yelks of 4 eggs, and 1 cupful sugar; whip it on fire until in state of high froth and a little thick; remove, and use as directed.

Sugar Sauce. — Beat to light cream ½ cupful sugar, flavored with ½ teaspoonful Royal Extract *Lemon*, and ½ cupful butter; add yelks of 2 eggs, and place on ice until wanted.

Spice Sauce. — Set on fire ¾ pint water, 1 cupful sugar; boil 20 minutes, remove from fire and add 1 teaspoonful each Royal Extract *Cloves* and *Ginger*.

Sauce Aux Quatre Fruits. —Remove very thinly one-third the rind of 1 lemon and 1 orange ; remove remainder with the thick white skin very close to pulp ; then cut each in small dice, removing seeds ; lay in bowl ; peel, core, and cut in dice 2 sour apples, which add to well made *Wine Sauce;* simmer until tender ; then add 1 cupful seedless raisins, lemon and orange dice, with lemon and orange peel, cut into shreds, and boil in very little water, which add to sauce to flavor ; when about to serve, add 1 teaspoonful Royal Extract *Almonds.*

Vanilla Sauce. --Put ½ pint milk in small saucepan over fire ; when scalding hot, add yelks 3 eggs ; stir until thick as boiled custard ; add, when taken from fire and cooled, 1 tablespoonful Royal Extract *Vanilla,* and whites of eggs whipped stiff.

Wine Sauce No. 1. —¾ pint water, 1 cupful sugar, 1 small teaspoonful corn starch, 1 teaspoonful each Royal Extract *Lemon* and *Cinnamon,* ½ gill wine. Boil water, add corn starch, dissolved in little cold water, and the sugar ; boil 15 minutes, strain ; when about to serve, add extracts and wine.

Wine Sauce No. 2. —½ pint water, 1 cupful sugar, ½ teaspoonful corn starch, 1 teaspoonful each Royal Extract *Bitter Almonds* and *Vanilla,* ½ cupful white wine. Stir 2 tablespoonfuls of sugar on the fire in thick saucepan, with 1 tablespoonful water, until very dark, *but not burned;* add water boiling, rest of sugar, the corn starch dissolved, boil 10 minutes ; when about to serve, strain, add extracts, and wine.

Custards, Tarts, Etc.

CUSTARDS require to be made carefully, and need not, unless occasion demands it, be made expensively. The plain boiled custard, usually served in with tarts or puddings, may be cheaply prepared.

Custards may have the delicate flavors of lemon, orange, rose, vanilla, nutmeg, etc., communicated to them by using Royal Flavoring Extracts. A few drops of *Rose* will answer where a teaspoonful or two of *Vanilla* would be required. By their use you avoid the necessity of straining the custard ; flavor should be used after boiling it to save driving off the fine aroma by the heat.

Banana Custard. — Make a white custard as follows : 2 tablespoonfuls corn starch, wetted with enough cold water to dissolve it ; 1 cup granulated sugar, ½ cup butter ; stir together in a pudding mould or earthen dish, and pour on enough boiling water to make thick custard ; heat the whites of three eggs to snow, stir into the custard, and set it in the oven to bake for 15 minutes, or for the same length of time in a pot of boiling water ; set aside until perfectly cold ; then remove the slight crust that will have formed on top ; have ready dish in which you are to serve your custard, and some fresh ripe bananas, minced finely ; mix with the custard and pour into the dish and add a meringue made of the beaten whites of 3 eggs, and ½ teacupful of pulverized pink sugar. A fine custard may be made according to above receipt by using peaches, instead of bananas, or Bartlett pears. Milk should never be used with acid fruits, particularly in warm weather, and pure cream in any quantity is a severe tax on a weak stomach. The custards for which formulas are given here can be made thus as real cream, answer the same purpose, are quite as palatable in most cases as the ordinary milk and cream, without danger of being curdled by the acidity of the fruit. Tapioca, arrowroot, etc., may be substituted for corn starch in the making of these custards, and pineapples, strawberries, raspberries, are delicious served in this way. Custards with an extra allowance of butter and a flavoring of Royal Extract *Vanilla, Almond* or *Rose,* make delicious cream pies. Bake with either 1 or 2 crusts of rich puff paste. If the former, add a

meringue. By using the yelks as well as the whites of eggs, and using the grated rind and juice of lemons and oranges, or both, delicious orange and lemon pies are made. These should be made with only one crust.

Banana Pie is made by using a white custard as above, and mixing with the pulp of ripe bananas, pressed through a colander or sieve, and baked in a rich open pastry crust, and finished with a meringue.

Chocolate Custards. Pour 2 tablespoonfuls of boiling water over 2 ounces of grated chocolate ; let it stand near the fire till perfectly dissolved. Put into pint of milk mixed with pint of cream, pinch of salt, and three ounces of sugar, simmer over fire 10 minutes ; then add by degrees yelks of 8 well-beaten eggs, and stir to a froth while it thickens ; then pour out to cool.

Plain Boiled Custard. —1 quart of milk, 8 eggs, peel of 1 large lemon, 3 laurel leaves, ½ pound of loaf sugar. Pour milk into clean saucepan with laurel leaves and peel of lemon, set at side of fire 20 minutes, when on point of boiling strain into basin to cool ; then stir in powdered sugar and well-beaten eggs ; again strain it into a jug, which place in deep saucepan of boiling water, and stir one way until it thickens ; then pour into glass dish or custard cups.

Vanilla Custard. —Boil 1 pint of cream with 4 ounces of sugar, for ¼ of an hour, then strain through muslin. Beat well yelks of 6 eggs, and pour milk over them into a bowl, placing bowl over pan of boiling water, and stirring rapidly till it thickens. Let it cool gradually ; add 1 teaspoonful Royal Extract *Vanilla* to suit taste, and stir continually. When cold serve in dish, covered with whipped white of eggs, sifted over with sugar.

Chocolate Blanc Mange. —Quart of milk, ½ box of gelatine, soaked in 1 cup of water ; four tablespoonfuls grated chocolate, rubbed smooth in a little milk ; 3 eggs, Royal Extract *Vanilla* to taste. Heat milk until boiling, then add other ingredients ; boil 5 minutes. Pour into mould. Serve cold with sugar and cream, or custard.

Tarts: Gooseberry, Currant, Apple or any Other Fruit. —Time to bake, from ¾ to 1 hour. 1 quart of gooseberries, rather more than 1½ lb. of paste, moist sugar to taste. Cut off tops and tails from gooseberries, or pick currants from their stalks, or pare and quarter the apples ; put them into pie-dish with sugar, line edge of dish with paste, pour in a little water, put on cover, ornament edge of paste in the usual manner, and bake it in a brisk oven.

Tartlets. —Time to bake, ¼ hour. Line some patty-pans with puff paste, fill them with any jam or preserve, and bake lightly.

Open Jam Tart. —Time to bake, until paste loosens from the dish. Line shallow tin dish with puff paste, put in the jam, roll out some of paste, wet it lightly with yelk of an egg beaten with a little milk, and a tablespoonful of powdered sugar. Cut it in very narrow strips, then lay them across the tart, lay another strip round the edge, trim off outside, and bake in quick oven.

Charlotte Russe. —2 tablespoonfuls gelatine soaked in a little cold milk 2 hours ; two coffee-cups rich cream ; one teacup milk. Whip cream stiff in large bowl or dish ; set on ice. Boil milk, and pour gradually over gelatine until dissolved, then strain ; when nearly cold add whipped cream, spoonful at a time. Sweeten with powdered sugar, flavor with Royal Extract *Vanilla.* Line dish with lady fingers or sponge cake ; pour in cream and set in cool place to harden.

Peaches and Cream. —Pare and slice the peaches just before sending to table. Cover the glass dish containing them to exclude the air as much as possible, as they soon change color Do not sugar them in dish—they then become preserves, not fresh fruit. Pass the powdered sugar and cream with them.

THE ROYAL BAKING POWDER IS ABSOLUTELY PURE.

Apple Meringue. – Spice and sweeten apple sauce ; heat in 2 or 3 eggs. Pour into pudding dish, bake quickly. When well crusted over, cover with meringue made by whipping whites of 3 eggs with a little sugar. Shut oven door and tinge slightly.

Meringues. – Whisk the whites of 4 eggs to high froth, then stir into it ½ pound finely powdered sugar; flavor with Royal Extract *Vanilla* or *Lemon*, repeat whisking until it will lie in a heap, then lay mixture on letter paper, in a shape of half an egg, moulding it with a spoon, laying each about half an inch apart. Then place paper containing meringues on piece of hard wood, put them into quick oven, do not close it, watch them ; when they begin to have yellow appearance, take out. Remove paper carefully from wood, let them cool for 2 or 3 minutes, then slip thin knife very carefully under one, turn it into your left hand, take another from paper in same way, join two sides which were next the paper together. The soft inside may be taken out with handle of small spoon, the shells filled with jam, jelly or cream, then joined together as above, cementing them with some of the mixture.

Iced Fruits for Desserts. – Any desirable fruit may be easily iced by dipping first in the beaten white of an egg, then in sugar finely pulverized, and again in egg, and so on until you have the icing of the desired thickness. For this purpose oranges or lemons should be carefully pared, and all the white inner skin removed that is possible, to prevent bitterness ; then cut either in thin horizontal slices if lemons, or in quarters if oranges. For cherries, strawberries, currants, etc., choose the largest and finest, leaving stems out. Peaches should be pared and cut in halves, and sweet juicy pears may be treated in the same way, or look nicely when pared, leaving on the stems, and iced. Pineapples should be cut in thin slices, and these again divided into quarters.

Floating Island. – 1 quart milk, 4 eggs. yelks and whites beaten separately, 4 tablespoonfuls sugar, 2 teaspoonfuls Royal Extract *Vanilla* or *Bitter Almonds;* ¼ cupful currant jelly. Heat milk to scalding, but not boiling. Beat the yelks ; stir into them the sugar, and pour upon them gradually, mixing well, a cup full of the hot milk. Return to saucepan and boil until it begins to thicken. When cool, flavor and pour into a glass dish. Heap upon top meringue of whites whipped until you can cut it, into which you have beaten the jelly, a teaspoonful at a time.

Jellies and Jams.

HOW TO MAKE JELLIES. – Put the fruit in stone jar placed in boiler of hot water. When fruit is sufficiently softened, strain through jelly-bag, place juice in preserving kettle and allow 1 pound of sugar to pint of juice. While heating juice place sugar in dish in oven ; allow juice to boil 20 minutes, then add heated sugar. Let all come to a boil and remove from fire ; having glasses scalded, pour in brimming full and allow them to stand in the sun for at least a day, or till jelly is thoroughly set ; cover with tissue paper saturated with brandy, and over all paste thick white or brown paper.

Apple Jelly. – Take apples, wipe and slice them ; use seeds, skins and all ; cook soft in cider enough to cover them ; strain through cloth laid in sieve ; add a pound of sugar to pint of juice and boil up a few minutes.

Currant Jelly. – 1 box (2 ounces) gelatine, dissolved in 1 pint cold water, 1 pint wine, 1 quart boiling water, 1 quart granulated sugar, and 3 lemons, grated.

Crab-apple Jelly. – Boil apples with just water enough to cover them until tender. Mash with spoon, and strain out juice. Take pint of juice to pound of sugar ; boil 30 minutes, strain through a hair sieve.

Calf's Feet Jelly. – Boil 2 calf's feet, well cleaned, in gallon of water till reduced to a quart, then pour into a pan. When cold, skim off all fat, take jelly up clean ; leave settlings at bottom ; put jelly into saucepan, with pint white wine, ½ pound loaf sugar, and juice of 4 lemons. Add the whites of 6 eggs, well beaten ; stir all well together, put on fire, let boil about 15 minutes without stirring. Pour into large flannel bag, repeat stirring until it runs clear ; then have ready large china basin.

Cider Jelly. – 1 box gelatine dissolved in 1 pint cold water. In 20 minutes add 1 pint boiling water, 1 quart cider, 1 pint sugar (granulated), and grated rind and juice of 2 lemons. Let stand on stove until hot, but do not boil. Then strain into moulds.

Plum Jelly. – Take as many plums as you have, pour sufficient boiling water over to cover them. Pour off water immediately, draining them. Put plums in preserving kettle with boiling water enough to cover again ; then boil till plums begin to open, and some juice is extracted. Then pour off liquid, strain it, add to each pound of juice 1 pound white sugar, return to kettle ; boil it from 20 minutes to ½ hour, as it may require, and you will have most delicious jelly. The plums may be used for pies or sauce.

Quince Jelly. – Slice quinces without either paring or coring. Put them into preserving kettle ; just cover with water ; put over fire, boil until soft. Remove from stove, strain off liquor. To every gallon allow 4 pounds white sugar ; boil very fast until it becomes a stiff jelly.

Lemon Jelly. – ½ box gelatine, soaked in ½ pint cold water 1 hour ; add 1 pint boiling water, and 1½ cups sugar, Royal Extract *Lemon* to taste. Stand on stove until boiling. Strain into mould. set in cool place.

Strawberry or Raspberry Jelly. – Get fine-colored, fresh, ripe fruit ; put over fire at sufficient distance for juice to flow slowly : do not allow it to run longer after it is perfectly clear, probably 20 minutes ; then run through jelly bag without pressing. If juice is at all turbid, strain again through muslin into pan, simmer it ¼ of an hour ; then add 1 pound fine sugar to each pint juice and boil 10 minutes longer.

Wine Jelly. – 1 package (2 ounces) gelatine, soaked 2 hours in a large cup cold water ; 2 cups white wine or sherry ; 1 lemon, all the juice and ½ the grated peel ; 1 teaspoonful Royal Extract *Bitter Almonds*, 2 cups white sugar, 2 cups boiling water. Put soaked gelatine, lemon, sugar, and Royal Extract together, and cover close ½ hour. Pour on boiling water, stir and strain. Add wine, and strain again through flannel bag, without squeezing, and leave in mould, wet with cold water until solid.

Black or Red Currant Jam. – Time, ¾ of an hour to 1 hour. To every pound of currants allow ¾ of a pound of sugar. Gather currants on fine day, pick from stalks. Put them into preserving pan with sugar broken into small pieces. Bring gradually to boil, then let simmer, removing scum as it rises, stirring jam constantly. When done, put into pots with brandy paper, or paper steeped in starch, over them, and tie them down closely.

Cherry Jam. – To 12 pounds cherries, when ripe, weigh 1 pound sugar : break the stones of part, and blanch them ; then put them to fruit and sugar ; boil all gently till jam comes clear from the pan.

Gooseberry Jam. – Time, 1¼ hours. ¾ pound loaf sugar to 1 pound red gooseberries. Pick off stalks and buds from gooseberries, bruise them lightly, boil them quickly for 8 or 10 minutes, stirring all the time ; then add sugar, pounded and sifted, to fruit, boil quickly, removing scum as it rises. Put into pots, when cold cover as above. All jams are made much in the same way.

Pineapple Jam. – Peel, grate, and weigh the apple. Put pound to pound of pineapple and sugar. Boil it in preserving kettle 30 or 40 minutes.

Preserves.

DIRECTIONS FOR PRESERVING FRUIT. — Preserves should be kept carefully from air, in very dry place ; if they stand in warm place they will mould. They should be looked at 2 or 3 times in first 2 months, that they may be gently boiled again if not likely to keep. It is supposed by some that cheap sugar will do for preserves ; this is a mistaken idea ; the very best sugar should be used ; if cheap sugar is used, it should be cleansed and skum all taken off.

Amount of Sugar to a Quart Jar.

Cherries	6	ounces
Strawberries	8	"
Raspberries	4	"
Lawton Blackberries	6	"
Field "	6	"
Quince	10	"
Sour Pears	8	"
Wild Grapes	8	"
Peaches	4	"
Bartlett Pears	6	"
Pineapples	6	"
Crab-apples	8	"
Plums	8	"
Pie Plant	10	"
Sour apples, quartered	6	"
Ripe Currants	8	"
Cranberries	12	"

Preparing Fruits for Preserving.

Boil Blackberries, moderately, about	6	minutes	
Plums,	"	10	"
Raspberries,	"	6	"
Cherries,	"	5	"
Strawberries,	"	8	"
Whortleberries,	"	5	"
Pie Plant, sliced,	"	10	"
Bartlett Pears, in halves,	"	20	"
Small sour Pears, whole,	"	30	"
Peaches, halves,	"	8	"
Peaches, whole,	"	15	"
Pineapple, sliced ½ in. thick,	"	15	"
Siberian or Crab apple, whole	"	25	"
Sour apples, quartered,	"	10	"
Ripe Currants,	"	6	"
Wild Grapes,	"	10	"
Tomatoes,	"	60	"

Pour into warm jars.

Citron Preserves. — Prepare rind into any form you desire, boil very hard 30 or 40 minutes in alum-water, tolerably strong ; take from alum water and put into clear cold water ; allow them to stand over night ; in morning change water and put them to boil ; let cook until they have entirely changed color and are quite soft ; then make syrup, allowing 1½ pounds white sugar to 1 pound fruit ; then add fruit, which needs but little more cooking. Mace, ginger or lemon flavors nicely.

Preserved Peaches. — Take ripe, but not soft peaches. Pour boiling water over them to take off skins, which will pull off easily. Weigh equal quantities fruit and sugar ; put them together in earthen pan over night. In morning pour off syrup, boil few minutes ; set off kettle, take off scum. Put back kettle on fire ; when syrup boils up, put in peaches. Boil them slowly ¾ of an hour ; take out and put in jars. Boil syrup 15 minutes more, and pour over them.

To Preserve Strawberries. — To one pound strawberries, after they have been picked over, add one pound clean sugar ; put them in preserving kettle, over slow fire, until sugar is melted, then boil them precisely 25 minutes fast as possible ; have jar ready and put fruit in boiling hot ; jar should be heated before hot fruit is poured into it, otherwise it will break. Cover and seal jars immediately ; set in a cool place.

Quince and Apple Preserves. — Take an equal amount of sweet apples and quinces ; weigh them, then take by weight an equal amount of sugar ; pare, quarter and core the fruit. When quince is boiled tender, take it out ; boil apples in quince water, put them into syrup, let them boil till they look red and clear — an hour and a half is not too long. Do not boil quinces in syrup, but put layers of the apple, when done, into jars with quince, previously cooked tender in water, and pour syrup over them.

Preserved Quinces. — Pare, quarter and core them, saving skins and cores. Put quinces over fire with just water enough to cover them, and simmer till soft, but do not let them cook till they break. Take out fruit and spread on dishes to cool ; add parings and cores to water in which quinces were boiled ; stew it an hour ; then strain through jelly-bag ; to each pint of this liquor allow a pound of sugar. Boil and skim this, put in fruit, and boil 15 minutes. Take all off the fire, and let stand in deep dish 24 hours. Then drain off syrup, let it boil, put in quinces, and boil 15 minutes. Take out fruit again, spread on dishes ; boil syrup down to a jelly, nearly. Put fruit into jars ¾ full, and cover with the syrup. The quinces will be a fine deep red color.

Ripe Tomato Preserves. — 7 pounds round yellow tomatoes peeled, 7 pounds sugar, juice 3 lemons, let stand together over night. Drain off syrup and boil it, skim well, then put in the tomatoes and boil gently 20 minutes. Take out fruit with skimmer, spread on dishes. Boil syrup down till it thickens, adding, just before you take it off fire, juice of the lemons. Put fruit into jars and fill up with hot syrup. When cold, seal up.

To Preserve Currants. — To 10 pounds currants, 7 pounds sugar ; take stems from 7 pounds currants, press the juice from other 3 pounds. When sugar is made into hot syrup, put in currants ; boil until thick and rich.

Utensils.

Absolutely required in a Kitchen.

1 Iron Pot. 1 Fish Kettle. 2 Large Iron Saucepans — one with a steamer. 1 Stewpan. 2 Small Saucepans for Vegetables. 2 Butter Saucepans. 1 Small Saucepan lined with china, for boiling milk. 1 Gridiron. 1 Frying-pan. 1 Roasting Jack and stand. 1 Bunch of Skewers. 1 Basting Ladle and slice. 1 Toasting Fork.

For Miners or Stockmen.

1 Iron Pot. 3 Saucepans. 1 Gridiron. 1 Frying-pan. Poor Man's Jack for toasting.

Soups and Broths.

BEEF SOUP No. 1. — Boil soup bone day before wanting it ; skim grease off next day, and melt jelly ; add spices to taste, little brandy, small teacupful of butter rubbed in browned flour, little vermicelli, and grated carrot. Boil 3 eggs hard, mash smooth, put in tureen, and pour soup over them.

Beef Soup No. 2. — Time, 9 hours ; 5 pounds of shin of beef, a quart of water to each pound of meat, 1 head celery, 1 onion, 4 small or 3 large carrots, 2 turnips, a bunch of sweet herbs, pepper and salt. Cut off meat from bone, put bone into stewpan with water, let boil slowly for 4 hours ; then strain into large basin ; when cold, remove cake of fat ; cut meat into small pieces, put them into stewpan with strained gravy, herbs tied together, celery, onions, carrots, and turnips cut small ; let simmer slowly for 5 hours, seasoning with pepper and salt to taste. When done, take out herbs, and it will be ready for use.

THE ROYAL BAKING POWDER IS ABSOLUTELY PURE.

Bouillon Soup. — 6 pounds of round of beef bound into a good shape with tape, 3 small carrots, 3 turnips, 8 small young onions, and one large one stuck with 4 cloves, bunch sweet herbs, 1 pint each string beans and peas, 1 small head cauliflower or cabbage, 4 quarts water, pepper, salt, noodles, rice or sago. Put beef whole in the water and heat slowly to a boil. Skim, dip out a pint of the liquor and put by for cooking the vegetables. Add to the liquor left with the beef 1 sliced carrot, 1 turnip also sliced, the large onion and the herbs; stew slowly 4 hours; take out the beef and keep hot over boiling water. Strain the soup, pulping the vegetables. Cool and skim, return to the fire and when it heats add noodles, boiled rice or soaked German sago. Simmer 5 minutes, and pour into the tureen.

Bean Soup. — Soak quart white beans over night; in morning pour off water; add fresh, and set over fire until skins will easily slip off; throw them into cold water, rub well, and skins will rise to top where they may be removed. Boil beans until perfectly soft, allowing 2 quarts water to 1 quart beans; mash beans, add flour and butter rubbed together, also salt and pepper. Cut cold bread into small pieces, toast and drop on soup when you serve.

Beef Tea. — 1 pound beef. Cut beef into small pieces like dice, put them in common preserve jar, keep in oven all day, or all night. When all juice of meat has been extracted by heat, add boiling water till it is of strength you require. Season to taste.

Family Soup. — Time, 6 hours; 3 or 4 quarts pot liquor, i. e. the water in which mutton or salt-beef has been boiled. Any bones from dressed meat, trimmings of poultry, scraps of meat or 1 pound gravy beef, 2 large onions 1 turnip, 2 carrots, a little celery seed tied in a piece muslin, bunch savory herbs, 1 sprig parsley, 5 cloves. 2 blades mace, a few peppercorns, pepper and salt to taste. Put all your meat trimmings, meat bones, etc., into stewpan. Stick onions with cloves, add them with other vegetables, to meat; pour over all the pot liquor; set over slow fire and let simmer gently, removing all scum as it rises. Strain through fine hair sieve.

French Soup. — Time, 3 hours; 3 quarts water, 4 pounds meat, 2 teaspoonfuls salt, 3 small carrots, 3 middling-sized onions (1 being stuck with 2 cloves), 1 head celery, 1 bunch Royal thyme, 1 bay leaf, little parsley tied together, 2 turnips, 1 burnt onion or a little browning. Put meat into stock-pot with water, set over slow fire and let it gently boil, carefully taking off scum that will rise to top. Pour in teacupful cold water to help scum to rise. When no more scum-rises, it is time to put in vegetables, which you should have ready washed and prepared. Cut carrots in slices, stick onions with cloves, cut turnips in 4 pieces. Put them into pot, let boil gently 2 hours. If water boils away too much, add a little hot water in addition. A few bones improve the soup very much.

Clam Soup. — Boil juice of clams, make a little drawn butter and mix with the juice; stir till it boils, chop up clams and put them in; season to taste with pepper, salt, and little lemon-juice; cream or milk and crackers are to be added, nutmeg if you like. Boil over slow fire 1½ hours.

Green Turtle Soup. — Take off shell, head, and flippers; let hang over night to drain off the blood; cook the neck and flippers in boiling water 1 minute, so that the scales can be scraped off. Take a 3-pound shin of beef, carrots, onions, whole black peppers, cloves, thyme, leeks, celery, and parsley to taste; cook in boiling water ¾ to 1 hour. Then cut the turtle in small pieces, leaving the liquid to cook with the bones and vegetables, adding 2 ounces butter and 3 tablespoonfuls flour to thicken the soup; simmer while cooking, and cook until it has lost the strong smell; then put in the meat (cut turtle and shin beef), season with red peppers, and 1 tablespoonful of sherry or brandy, and then serve.

Chicken Broth. — Cut fowl into quarters. Lay it in salt and water an hour; put on in soup kettle with an onion and 4 quarts water. Bring very slowly to gentle boil and keep this up until liquid has diminished ½ and meat shrinks from bones. Take out chicken, salt it and set aside with cupful of broth, in bowl (covered), until next day. Season rest of broth and put back over fire. Boil up and skim, add nearly cupful of rice, previously soaked in bowl of water. Cook slowly until rice is tender. Stir cupful hot milk into 2 beaten eggs, then into broth. Let all come barely to a boil. When you have added handful of finely minced parsley, pour out into tureen and serve.

Consommé Soup. — 1 chicken, 3 pounds lean beef, 1 onion, 1 turnip, 2 carrots, bunch sweet herbs, 7 quarts cold water, ½ cup sago soaked in cold water, pepper and salt. Cut beef in strips and joint chicken, slice vegetables, chop herbs, put all on with water to cook slowly for 6 hours. Take out chicken and beef; salt and pepper and put into jar. Strain soup, pulping vegetables through a sieve. Season and divide it, pouring ½ on meat in jar, and setting in pot hot water to cook, covered, 2 hours more. Heat the rest and skim; put in sago, simmer for ½ hour, then pour out. When 2 hours have passed, pour out stock in bowl; when cold put on ice.

Tomato Soup. — Skin carefully 1 gallon ripe tomatoes, put them in soup-pot, pour over 2 quarts rich soup stock. Let simmer an hour, run through sieve, return to pot, season with pepper, salt and clove of garlic; dish soup as soon as it boils up second time.

Mock Turtle Soup. — 1 calf's head, 2 onions, 1 bunch sweet herbs, 5 tablespoonfuls butter, 5 tablespoonfuls browned flour, 1 tablespoonful allspice, ½ teaspoonful mace, 1 teaspoonful pepper, about 2 teaspoonfuls salt, 2 raw eggs, a little flour, 2 glasses brown sherry, or Madeira wine, 1 tablespoonful mushroom or walnut catsup, 5 quarts cold water, 1 sliced lemon, 1 calf's head, well cleaned, with the skin on. Soak the head 1 hour in cold water and boil in 5 quarts water until the bones will slip easily from the flesh. Take out the head, leave bones and broth in the pot. Take out the tongue and brains and put on separate plates; set aside also the cheeks and fleshy parts to cool. Chop the rest, including the ears, very fine. Reserve 4 tablespoonfuls of this for force-meat balls. Season the rest with pepper, salt, onion, allspice, herbs and mace and put back into the pot, cover close and cook for 4 hours. Should liquor sink to less than 4 quarts replenish with boiling water. Just before straining the soup take out ½ cupful put into a frying-pan, heat and stir in the browned flour wet up in cold water, also the butter. Simmer these together 10 minutes, stirring constantly. Strain the soup, scald the pot and return the broth to the fire. Have ready the tongue and fleshy parts of the head, cut, after cooling, into small squares, also about 15 balls made of the chopped meat, highly seasoned, worked into proper consistency with a little flour and bound with the raw eggs, beaten into paste. They should be as soft as can be handled. Grease pie plate, flour the balls and set in quick oven until crust forms upon them, then cool. Now thicken the strained broth with the mixture in the frying-pan, stirred in well. If not sufficient to make it almost like custard add more flour. Then drop in the dice of tongue and fat meat, cook slowly 5 minutes. Put the force-meat balls and thin slices of a peeled lemon into the tureen. Pour the soup upon them, add catsup and wine, cover 5 minutes and serve. Mock turtle soup is regarded as the queen of all soups, and far superior to turtle soup.

Potato Soup (4 quarts). — Put in saucepan 2 ounces bacon chopped, 6 onions peeled and chopped, 1 saltspoonful pepper, 1 teaspoonful salt, and 4 quarts hot water, boil 15 minutes; meantime peel and slice 1 quart potatoes, add them to first-mentioned ingredients, boil ¾ hour longer, or until potatoes are boiled to a pulp; season palatably, serve hot.

Green Pea Soup.—Put 2 quarts green peas with 4 quarts water, boil 2 hours, keeping steam waste supplied by fresh boiling water—strain them from liquor, return that to pot, rub the peas through sieve, chop an onion fine, and small sprig mint, let boil 10 minutes, stir a tablespoonful flour into 2 of butter, add pepper and salt to taste, stir smoothly into boiling soup. Serve with well buttered sippets of toasted bread.

Macaroni, or Vermicelli Soup.—2 small carrots, 4 onions, 2 turnips, 2 cloves, 1 tablespoonful salt; pepper to taste. Royal herbs—marjoram, parsley and thyme. Any cooked or uncooked meat. Put soup bones in enough water to cover; when they boil, skim, add the vegetables. Simmer 3 or 4 hours, strain through colander and put back in saucepan to reheat. Boil ½ pound macaroni until quite tender, place in soup tureen, and pour soup over it—the last thing. Vermicelli will only need to be soaked a short time—not boiled.

Scotch Mutton Broth.—Time, 3½ hours; 6 lbs. neck of mutton, 3 quarts water, 5 carrots, 5 turnips, 2 onions, 4 tablespoonfuls Scotch barley, a little salt. Soak mutton in water for an hour, cut off scrag, and put it in stewpan with 3 quarts of water. As soon as it boils skim well and then simmer for 1½ hours. Cut best end of mutton into cutlets, dividing it with 2 bones in each; take off nearly all fat before you put it into broth; skim the moment meat boils, and every 10 minutes afterwards; add carrots, turnips and onions, all cut into 2 or 3 pieces, then put them into soup soon enough to be thoroughly done; stir in Scotch barley; add salt to taste, let all stew together for 3½ hours; about ½ an hour before sending it to table, put in little chopped parsley and serve.

Soup Stock or Clear Soup.—5 pounds of beef from the round, 5 quarts of water, 1 onion, 3 stalks of celery, herbs, 6 cloves, salt and pepper. Put the beef (which must be lean) and the water on the fire, and let it boil slowly 8 hours; skim it, and strain; when cold, take off the fat, then add the vegetables, etc., seasoning, boil gently 20 minutes, strain through a cloth. This is now ready for clear soup, or stock for any other kind.

Ox-Tail Soup.—1 ox-tail, 2 pounds lean beef, 4 carrots, 3 onions, thyme and parsley, pepper and salt to taste, 4 quarts cold water. Cut tail into joints, fry brown in good dripping. Slice onions and two carrots and fry in the same, when you have taken out the pieces of tail. When done tie them, the thyme and parsley in lace bag, and drop into the soup pot. Put in the tail, then the beef cut into strips. Grate over them 2 whole carrots, pour over all the water and boil slowly 4 hours; strain and season; thicken with brown flour wet with cold water; boil 15 minutes longer and serve.

Oyster Stew.—Take the oysters with their liquor, adding a little water, if not sufficient liquor; 1 tablespoonful butter, pepper and salt to taste; cover the stewpan; place over fire, then remove as soon as it boils; if milk is desired, the bottom of the soup plates should simply be covered with cold milk, then serve the stew.

NOTE.—Many prefer oysters well done, in which case stew should be boiled 5 minutes.

Fish.

DIRECTIONS FOR COOKING.—Clean your fish carefully, slit it low enough so as not to have any blood on the backbone, but do not make too large a cut so as to spoil look of fish. The sound adheres to bone, and must be left, so must the hard and soft roes; care must be taken not to break liver, which in most fish is replaced; great care must be taken not to break gall, for it would make fish bitter. Never fry fish in butter; fry them in good dripping or lard—oil is best, but it is very expensive.

To Broil Fish.—Clean, wash, and wipe dry. Split, so that when laid flat, the backbone will lie in the middle. Sprinkle with salt and lay, inside down, upon a buttered gridiron over a clear fire until it is nicely colored, then turn. When done, put upon a hot dish, butter plentifully, and pepper. Put a hot cover over it and send to table.

Broiled Fresh Cod.—Sew up the piece of fish in thin cloth, fitted to shape, boil in salted water (boiling from the first), allow about 15 minutes to the pound. Carefully unwrap, and pour over it sauce for codfish. See Sauces.

Boiled Bass, or Other Fish.—Put sufficient water in pot to enable fish, if alive, to swim easily. Add ½ cup vinegar, 1 teaspoonful salt, 1 onion, 1 dozen whole black peppers, 1 blade mace. Sew up fish in piece of clean net or muslin, fitted to shape. Heat slowly for first ½ hour; then boil 8 minutes, at least, to pound, quite fast. Unwrap, and pour over it cup of drawn butter based upon the liquor in which fish was boiled, with juice of ½ lemon stirred into it.

Baked Fish.—A fish weighing from 4 to 6 pounds is good size to bake. It should be cooked whole to look well. Make dressing of bread crumbs, butter, salt, and a little salt pork chopped fine (parsley and onions, if you please); mix this with 1 egg. Fill the body, sew it up, lay in large dripper; put across it some strips of salt pork to flavor it. Put pint water and little salt in pan. Bake an hour and a half. Baste frequently. After taking up fish, thicken gravy and pour over it.

CREAM GRAVY FOR BAKED FISH.—Have ready in saucepan 1 cup cream, diluted with a few spoonfuls hot water; stir in carefully 2 tablespoonfuls melted butter and a little chopped parsley; heat this in vessel filled with hot water. Pour in gravy from dripping pan of fish. Boil thick.

Broiled Salt Mackerel.—Freshen by soaking it over night in water, taking care that the skin lies uppermost. In the morning dry it without breaking, cut off the head and tip of the tail, place it between the bars of a buttered fish gridiron, and broil to a light brown; lay it on a hot dish, and dress with a little butter, pepper and lemon juice, vinegar, or chopped pickle.

Broiled Salt Salmon or Other Salt Fish.—Soak salmon in tepid or cold water 24 hours, changing water several times, or let stand under faucet of running water. If in a hurry or desiring a very salt relish, it may do to soak short time, having water warm, and changing, parboiling slightly. At the hour wanted, broil sharply. Season to suit taste, covering with butter. This receipt will answer for all kinds of salt fish. (For Salmon Sauce see Sauces.)

Broiled Halibut.—Slices of halibut, salt, pepper, butter. Cut the slices of fish about an inch thick, season with pepper and salt, and lay them in melted butter ½ hour, allowing 3 tablespoonfuls of butter to a pound of fish, then roll them in flour, and broil about 20 minutes. Serve very hot.

Codfish Balls.—Put fish in cold water, set on back of stove; when water gets hot, pour off and put on cold again until fish is fresh enough; then pick it up. Boil potatoes and mash them; mix fish and potatoes together while potatoes are hot, taking ⅔ potatoes and ⅓ fish. Put in plenty of butter; make into balls and fry in plenty of lard. Have lard hot before putting in balls.

Fried Blue Fish, and other Kinds.—Clean, wipe dry, inside and out. Sprinkle with flour, and season with salt. Fry in hot butter or sweet lard, ½ lard and ½ butter make a good mixture for frying fish. The moment fish are done to good brown, take them from fat and drain in hot strainer; garnish with parsley.

To Fry Brook Trout or any other Small Fish.—Clean fish, and let them lie few minutes wrapped singly in clean dry towel; season with pepper and salt; roll in corn meal, fry in ½ butter and ⅔ lard; drain on sieve, and serve hot.

THE ROYAL BAKING POWDER IS ABSOLUTELY PURE.

Fish Chowder. — Cut 2 or 3 slices of salt pork into dice pieces; fry to crisp, and turn the whole into chowder kettle. Pare 6 medium sized potatoes and cut them in two. Peel small onion and chop fine. Put potatoes into kettle with part of onion. Cut fish (which should be fresh cod or haddock) into convenient pieces, and lay over potatoes; sprinkle over it rest of the onion. Season well with salt and pepper, add just enough water to come to top of fish. Pour over the whole quart can tomatoes; cover closely and allow about as long to cook as takes to boil potatoes; then add 2 quarts milk, and let it scald up again. Season with *Sauce Piquant* or tomato catsup and more salt and pepper if required.

Fish Cake. — 1. Put bones of fish, with head and fins, into stewpan, with about a pint of water, add pepper and salt to taste; 1 good sized onion, handful sweet herbs, if you like; stew all slowly about 2 hours. Then mince fine clear meat of fish, mixing well with bread crumbs and cold mashed potatoes, and small quantity finely chopped parsley; season with salt and pepper to taste, make whole into cake with an egg well beaten. Brush it over lightly with white of egg, strew with bread crumbs and fry rich amber brown. Strain gravy made from bones, etc., and pour it over; stir gently for 10 minutes or ¼ hour. Serve very hot, with garnish of parsley and lemon slices. 2. Carefully remove bones and skin from fish left from dinner, and put it into warm water for short time. After taking it out press dry and beat in mortar to fine paste, with equal quantity of mashed potatoes; season to taste. Then make up the mass into round flat cakes, fry them in butter or lard till they are of fine golden brown color. Be sure they do not burn. Codfish is excellent recooked after this fashion.

Shell Fish.

CLAM CHOWDER. 25 clams, ½ pound salt pork, chopped fine, 6 potatoes sliced thin, 4 onions sliced thin. Put pork in kettle; after cooking a short time add potatoes, onions and juice of clams. Cook 2½ hours, then add clams; 15 minutes before serving add 2 quarts milk.

Clam Fritters. — 50 small or 25 large clams; dry them in napkin. If large, cut them in two; put pint of flour into basin, add two well beaten eggs, ½ pint milk, and nearly as much of clam liquor; beat batter till free from lumps, then stir in clams. Put lard or beef drippings into frying pan, heat it to boiling, then drop in clam batter by spoonful. Fry brown on one side, then turn and fry on the other.

Fricassee of Oysters. — Set 75 oysters on the fire with their liquor and equal quantity of chicken broth, 1 glass white wine, 2 blades mace; when they boil remove from fire and then from boiling *braise*, which return to fire; in clean stewpan put piece of butter size of an egg, 1½ tablespoonfuls flour; stir 5 minutes where it will not color, add to it the liquor, stir 5 minutes, then add yelks 5 eggs; 1 saltspoonful white pepper and salt, 1 tablespoonful chopped parsley; don't let boil; make the oysters hot in it; use as directed.

Fried Oysters. — Select largest and finest oysters. Drain and wipe them by spreading upon cloth, laying another over them, pressing lightly. Roll each in beaten egg, then in cracker crumbs with which have been mixed a very little pepper. Fry in mixture of equal parts of lard and butter.

Pickled Oysters. — 2 gallons of large oysters, drain and rinse them; put 1 pint of oyster juice in 1 quart of vinegar over fire; scald and skim until clear; add 1 tablespoonful whole pepper, 1 tablespoonful cloves, 1 tablespoonful mace, 1 even tablespoonful salt; scald a minute, then throw in oysters; let them just come to a boil. The oysters should be pickled day before being wanted, as they grow tough after standing a few days in vinegar.

Oyster Patés. — 1 quart oysters, minced fine with a sharp knife; 1 cup rich drawn butter based upon milk; cayenne and black pepper to taste. Stir minced oysters in drawn butter and cook 5 minutes. Have ready some shapes of pastry, baked in paté-pans, then slipped out. Fill these with the mixture; set in oven 2 minutes to heat, and send to table.

Scalloped Oysters. — 1 quart fine oysters, 1 coffeecupful pounded cracker, 2 tablespoonfuls butter, ½ cupful rich milk or cream. Pepper and salt to taste. Butter a baking dish and cover bottom pretty thickly with pounded cracker. Wet with oyster liquor and few spoonfuls cream, next lay oysters, 1 deep, closely over these. Pepper and salt, and small piece of butter on each. Another layer of crumbs, wet as before, more oysters; proceed in same way until dish is full, making top layer of crumbs, with butter dotted over it. Set in oven, invert plate or tin pan over dish, bake until juice bubbles up to top. Uncover, set upon upper grating of oven to brown. Serve in bake dish. Pass around sliced lemon with it. Oysters, like fish, follow immediately after soup, and are a course by themselves.

Oyster Pie. — 1 quart of oysters, drained; pepper, salt and butter to taste. 1 quart flour, 2 tablespoonfuls lard, 1 tablespoonful salt, mix with water for pie crust. Butter plate, then line pie plate with crust; fill with oysters, seasoned; put over a crust, and bake.

To Boil Lobsters or Crabs. — The lobster is in good season from September to June, and should be purchased alive and plunged into boiling water in which a good proportion of salt has been mixed. Continue to boil, according to size, from 20 minutes to an hour. Crabs should be boiled in the same manner, but a little more than half the time is necessary.

Deviled Crabs. — 1 cup crab meat, picked from shells of well boiled crabs, 2 tablespoonfuls fine bread crumbs or rolled cracker, yelks of two hard boiled eggs chopped, juice of a lemon, ½ teaspoonful mustard, a little cayenne pepper and salt, 1 cup good drawn butter. Mix 1 spoonful crumbs with chopped crab meat, yelks, seasoning, drawn butter. Fill scallop shells — large clam shells will do — or small paté-pans — with the mixture; sift crumbs over top, heat to slight browning in quick oven.

Soft Shell Crabs. — Fry in butter or lard.

Deviled Lobster. — 1 can preserved lobster, 3 tablespoonfuls butter, 4 tablespoonfuls vinegar, ½ teaspoonful made mustard, 1 good pinch cayenne pepper, boiled eggs for garnishing, salt. Empty contents lobster can into bowl 1 hour before using it. Mince evenly. Put vinegar, butter and seasoning into saucepan; when it simmers add lobster. Cook slowly, covered, ½ hour, stirring occasionally. Turn into deep dish, and garnish with slices of egg.

Lobster Patés. — Make puff paste and spread on very deep paté-pans. Bake it empty. Having boiled well 2 or 3 fine lobsters, extract all the meat and mince very small, mixing it with coral smoothly mashed and yelk of hard-boiled egg, grated. Season with a little salt, cayenne, and powdered mace or nutmeg, adding a little yellow lemon rind, grated. Moisten mixture well with cream, fresh butter, or salad oil. Put it into stewpan, add very little water, let stew till it just comes to a boil. Take off the fire, and the patés being baked, remove them from tin pans, place them on large dish, and fill them up to top with the mixture. Similar patés may be made of prawns or crabs.

Meats.

Broiling. — The rules for roasting meat apply to broiling, except that instead of cooking it in the oven it is to be quickly browned first on one side and then on the other, over a hot fire, and removed a little from the fire to finish cooking. Meat an inch thick will broil in about 20 minutes. It should be seasoned after it is cooked.

BOILING AND STEWING. — Fresh meat for boiling should be put into boiling water and boiled very gently about 20 minutes for each pound. A little salt, spice or vegetables may be boiled in the water with the meat for seasoning. A little vinegar put in the water with tough meat makes it tender. The broth of boiled meat should always be saved to use in soups, stews and gravies. Stewing and simmering meats mean to place them near enough to the fire to keep the water on them bubbling moderately, constantly and slowly. Salt meats should be put over the fire in cold water, and that as soon as it boils should be replaced by fresh cold water, the water to be changed until it remains fresh enough to give the meat a palatable flavor when done. Salted and smoked meats require about 30 minutes very slow boiling, from the time the water boils, to each pound. Vegetables and herbs may be boiled with them to flavor them. When they are cooked the vessel containing them should be set where they will keep hot without boiling until required if they are to be served hot; if they are to be served cold they should be allowed to cool in the pot liquor in which they were boiled. Very salt meats, or those much dried in smoking, should be soaked over night in cold water before boiling.

FRYING. — There are two distinct methods of frying, one with very little fat in the pan. To practice this successfully, the pan and fat must be hot before the article to be fried is put into it: for instance, in frying chops, if the pan is hot, and only fat enough is used to keep the chops from sticking to it, the heat being maintained so that the chops cook quickly, they will be nearly as nice as if they were broiled. Frying by the other method consists in entirely immersing the article to be cooked in sufficient smoking hot fat to cover it, and keeping the fat at that degree of heat until the food is brown. It should then be taken up with a skimmer and laid upon brown paper for a moment to free it from grease.

BREADED MUTTON CHOPS. — Trim neatly, cut off all fat and skin, roll in beaten egg, then in cracker crumbs, and fry in hot dripping. Turn as the under side browns, drain and serve.

Roast Beef. — Rib roast is best. Have butcher saw off about ½ bone. Cut ends of ribs clear of meat; fold flap neatly around to thick part, and secure with skewers. The trimmings are yours. As meat is weighed first, take it all — will make good material for soup or gravy. Put beef in dripping pan; pour cup of boiling water over it. Rub a little salt into fat parts: roast 10 minutes for every pound. Bake soon as juice begins to flow. If meat has much fat on top cover fatty portion with paste made of flour and water. When nearly done remove this, dredge beef with flour; baste well with gravy. Sprinkle salt over top and serve. Pour fat from gravy, return to fire, thicken with browned gravy, season and boil up once. Roast most all other meats in same way.

To Roast a Sirloin of Beef. — Time, ¼ of an hour to each 1 pound of meat. Make up good fire; spit or hang joint evenly at short distance from it; put a little clarified dripping in pan, baste the joint well soon as it is put down to dress; baste again every 1½ of an hour till about 20 minutes before it is done; then stir fire and make it clear; sprinkle a little salt, dredge a little flour over the meat, turn again till it is brown and frothed. Take from the spit, put on hot dish, pour over it some well made gravy, or mix the gravy left at bottom of dripping pan with a little hot water, and pour it over it. Garnish with fine scrapings of horse-radish in little heaps. Serve Yorkshire pudding with it on separate dish.

Beef's Tongue. — Wash a large perfectly fresh tongue in 3 waters; then cover well with boiling water, a little salt, and cook about 12 minutes to the pound. Strip off the skin. Dish when you have trimmed away the root, and pour over following sauce: Strain cup of the liquor in which tongue was boiled; set over fire, and stir in 2 tablespoonfuls butter cut up in flour, pepper to taste, the juice of 1 lemon, and when this has thickened, 2 small pickled cucumbers chopped, and serve.

Beefsteak Pie (French Style). — Take a nice piece of beef, rump or sirloin, cut in small slices; slice also a little raw ham; put both in a frying-pan, with some butter and small quantity chopped onions; let them simmer together a short time on the fire or in the oven; add a little flour and enough stock to make sauce; salt, pepper, chopped parsley and a little Worcestershire sauce as seasoning; add also a few sliced potatoes, and cook together for about 20 minutes; put this into a pie-dish, with a few slices of hard boiled eggs on the top, and cover with a layer of common paste. Bake from 15 to 20 minutes in a well heated oven. All dark meat pies can be treated precisely the same way. If poultry, leave the potatoes out.

Beefsteak Pudding No. 1. — *Paste No. 2.* 2½ pounds round steak, 1 level teaspoonful each Royal celery salt, Royal thyme, and marjoram, 1 small onion, salt and white pepper to taste, 4 sprigs parsley. Line well buttered pudding mould with the paste, wet edges, make layer of beef, cut in neat scallops, sprinkle with onion and parsley minced very fine, mixed on plate with celery salt, thyme, marjoram, salt, and pepper; then another layer of beef, and seasoning, and so on until each is used; fill up with cold water, cover it in with paste, place buttered paper over, set in saucepan with boiling water to reach two-thirds up outside of mould; steam thus 2½ hours, turn carefully out on dish, pour over it gravy that may be at hand, made hot and flavored with any kind of *Sauce Piquante.*

Broiled Steak. — Time, 8 to 10 minutes. Rump steak, 1 ounce butter, pepper and salt. Rump steak is best for broiling and frying; beef steak for stewing. Have steak cut about ¾ or ½ inch in thickness; place gridiron over clear fire and rub bars with fat. Place steak on it and broil, turning frequently, *carefully* pricking fork through fat, for if steak itself is pricked gravy will run out, and it will harden. Have ready hot dish on which you have placed lump of butter size of large walnut, catsup, pepper and salt. Lay steak (rubbing lightly over with butter) on dish; serve quickly as possible.

Braised Beef. — Put piece beef fillet without bone, weighing 5 or 6 pounds, in a pot. Scatter sliced onions over it, salt slightly, and if you have any good gravy add it to the cup of boiling water you pour over the meat. Cover lightly; cook slowly 1½ hours. Add more boiling water should gravy sink too low. When done dredge with flour; set in a hot oven. As the flour browns baste with butter to glaze. It should not remain longer in oven than ten minutes. Strain the gravy; pour on the fat; put into saucepan with a little browned flour and a tablespoonful of catsup. Boil until thickened, pour few teaspoonfuls over the meat, and serve rest in a boat.

To Mince Beef. — Shred the underdone part fine, with some of the fat; put it into a small stewpan, with some onions (a very little will do), a little water, pepper and salt. Boil it till the onion is quite soft, and then put some of the gravy of the meat to it, and the mince. Do not let it boil. Have a small hot dish with bits of bread ready, and pour the mince into it, but first mix a large spoonful of vinegar with it.

Bacon and Eggs. — Cut bacon in thin slices and fry it. When bacon is done fry eggs in same pan. Break each egg separately in a cup, then throw quickly into pan. Lay fried egg on each slice of bacon.

Broiled Beefsteak. — Flatten with the broad side of a hatchet, and broil upon a buttered gridiron over a clear fire; lay upon a hot dish, pepper, salt, and put a large spoonful butter cut in small bits upon it. Cover with a hot dish for 5 minutes before it is carved.

Broiled Ham and Poached Eggs. — Cut slices of boiled ham of equal size; broil on a gridiron over a clear fire; lay on a hot dish. Lay on each a poached egg, neatly trimmed, and serve.

To Boil a Ham. — Time 4 or 5 hours. A blade of mace, a few cloves, a sprig of thyme, and 2 bay leaves. Well soak ham in large quantity of water for 24 hours, then trim and scrape very clean; put into large stewpan, with more than sufficient water to cover it; put in mace, cloves, thyme, and bay leaves. Boil for 4 or 5 hours, according to weight; when done, let it become cold in liquor in which it was boiled. Then remove rind carefully, without injuring the fat; press cloth over it to absorb as much of the grease as possible; shake some bread-raspings over the fat. Serve cold garnished with parsley. Ornament knuckle with paper frill.

Boiled Ham. — Boil it 3 or 4 hours, according to size, then skin the whole and fit it for the table; then set in oven for ½ an hour, cover thickly with pounded rusk or bread crumbs, set back for ½ an hour longer. Boiled ham is always improved by setting in an oven for nearly an hour, till much of the fat dries out, and it also makes it more tender.

Boiled Corned Beef and Turnips. — Select a piece not too salt. The brisket is a good cut for family use when not too fat. Cook beef in plenty cold water. Bring slowly to boil. Cook 18 minutes to the pound after it begins to simmer. When fully ¾ done put in a dozen turnips, peeled and quartered. When both beef and turnips are thoroughly done dish out the beef, and lay the turnips unmashed about it. Serve with drawn butter, having as a base the pot liquor. Remaining liquor will make a good soup for next day's dinner.

Boiled Pigs Feet. — Wash 12 pigs feet clean, place in deep pan, and pour scalding water over them; take them out, light piece paper and burn hair off each one in same manner as a fowl is cleaned, then place them in warm water; boil slowly 1½ hours, or until tender; then put them in vinegar, let simmer very slowly for another ½ hour; fill small muslin bag with equal portions of cloves and allspice, bag to be size of an egg, tie up and drop in the pig's feet and vinegar; let all boil up for 10 minutes, salt to taste.

Boiled Mutton. — Put on in plenty of boiling water, salted; cook 12 minutes to the pound; take out, wipe carefully with a hot wet cloth; butter all over, and serve with a cup of drawn butter sent up in sauceboat.

Croquettes of Sweetbreads. — Blanch and braize 1 dozen sweetbreads. When cooked, cut them in small square pieces, also ½ can of mushrooms. Put in saucepan to cook, 2 finely chopped shalots or garlic with piece of butter; add some Allemande sauce, reduce it, then add sweetbreads and mushrooms. Season with salt, pepper, nutmeg and a little chopped parsley, add the yelks of 2 eggs, stir well, then put in pan to cool. Shape them in any desired form; bread them with bread crumbs, fry in hot lard. Serve with mushroom or cream sauce. You may add beef tongues or truffles, cut in small squares.

Mutton Chops Broiled. — Cut some chops from the best end of the loin or neck, trim them neatly, removing the skin or fat, leaving only enough of the latter to make them palatable. Place the chops on a gridiron over a very clear fire; turn them frequently, taking care that the fork is not put into the lean part of the chops. Season them with pepper and salt. When done put a piece of fresh butter over each chop, and send them to the table on a hot dish. Pork chops are cooked in the same manner. Time, 10 minutes.

Elk or Venison Steak. — Beat and prepare steak. Have ready 2 or 3 slices of breakfast bacon. Put steak on very hot frying-pan. Lay slices of bacon on top. When brown turn, and continue to do so until done to taste. Pepper, salt, and serve hot.

Lamb Cutlets. — Trim carefully; lay in a little warm butter for an hour, turning several times; then broil on a greased gridiron, taking care they do not drip; butter, pepper and salt each, lay in circle on plate, and serve.

Liver and Bacon. — 3 lbs. fresh liver, 1 lb. streaked bacon, juice of one lemon, one tablespoonful each flour and butter, 1 onion, and pepper and salt. Soak liver in cold water 20 minutes, wipe dry and cut in medium strips. Cut as many very thin strips of bacon and fry the bacon 3 minutes in its own fat. Salt, pepper and dredge the liver and flour before it goes in. When it is done lay in two rows the length of dish, with a strip of bacon between each piece of liver. Strain the fat, and return to the pan with a cupful of hot water, the butter rubbed into the flour, and when it has boiled up the juice of lemon; pour over the liver. Pass mustard with this dish.

Leg of Mutton Roasted. — Time, ¼ hour or 20 minutes to each pound. A leg of mutton intended for roasting can be kept much longer than for boiling, but must be wiped very dry, and dusted with flour and pepper. Cut off knuckle, remove thick skin, and trim off piece of thick flank. Put a little salt and water into dripping-pan, baste joint for short time with it, then use gravy from meat itself, basting every 10 minutes. Serve with gravy poured round it. The wether leg of mutton is best for roasting. A leg of mutton, if too large, can be divided, and knuckle boiled. By placing a paste of flour and water over part cut off, to keep in gravy, it can be roasted, by which means two roast dinners can be had from one joint.

Mutton Chops, Larded. — Trim off superfluous fat and skin, beat each chop flat, and lard each with strips of fat salt pork, drawn quite through so as to protect both sides of the chop. Put into saucepan, sprinkle with minced onion, pepper and parsley, and barely cover with any weak broth you may chance to have. Put on the saucepan lid; set it where it will not boil under 1 hour. Then increase heat and simmer ½ hour, or until tender. Take up the chops and keep hot. Thicken gravy with browned flour, add juice of 1 lemon, 1 large spoonful mushroom catsup, 1 glass sherry wine and stir 1 minute. Put back the chops and heat to a weak boil. Lay chops on dish, pour over the gravy and serve.

Pigeon Pie. — Clean, wash, and cut pigeons into quarters, wipe dry, and fry lightly in butter or dripping. Sprinkle well with salt and pepper. Have ready a greased pudding-dish and a good paste. Lay some pieces of pigeon in the bottom of the dish, and cover with a mixture of chopped eggs and the giblets boiled tender in a little water and then minced. More pigeon and another layer of the force-meat. Stir 2 tablespoonfuls of butter, rolled in flour, into the hot water in which the giblets were boiled. Season and pour enough into the pie to half cover the birds. Cover with a thick crust with slit in middle. Bake in 1 hour if pie be of fair size. Glaze with beaten egg just before it is taken from oven.

Roast Rabbits. — Skin and clean with great care, and wash a pair of fat rabbits (or hares), stuff with a force-meat of crumbs and chopped fat pork, seasoned with onion, thyme, pepper and salt. Sew up with fine thread, bind the legs to the body in a kneeling posture, and place in dripping pan. Pour over them 1 cupful boiling water, and invert another pan over them to keep them in. Baste with butter twice, with their own gravy twice, and twice again with butter. Just before you take them up dredge with flour and give a final baste with butter. Dish when threads have been cut and drawn out. Thicken and season the gravy. Serve in gravy-boat.

Pork Chops, with Tomate Gravy.—Trim off skin and fat; rub the chops over with a mixture of powdered sage and onion; put small piece butter into a frying-pan; put in the chops and cook slowly, as they should be well done. Lay chops on hot dish; add a little hot water to gravy in pan; 1 large spoonful butter, rolled in flour; pepper, salt and sugar, and ½ cup juice drained from can tomatoes. The tomatoes themselves can be used for a tomato omelette. Stew 5 minutes and pour over the chops and serve.

Roast Pig.—Take a young pig. After thoroughly cleaning inside, rinse it out with table soda and water, then again with cold water, wiping pig dry inside and out. Prepare following dressing: 1 cupful crumbs, ½ onion (chopped), 2 teaspoonfuls powdered sage, 3 tablespoonfuls melted butter, 1 saltspoonful salt, same pepper, ½ nutmeg (grated), and yelks of 2 eggs well beaten, moisten with ½ cup soup stock, stuff pig into its original size and shape, sew up, place in kneeling posture in dripping pan, tying the legs in proper position; dredge with flour; pour a little hot salted water in dripping pan; baste with butter and water 3 times as the pig warms; afterwards with gravy from dripping pan. When it begins to smoke all over, rub every 20 minutes with rag dipped in melted butter. This will keep skin from cracking. Roast in moderate steady oven 2 hours. Place the pig upon a large hot dish, surround with parsley and blanched celery tops, place a green wreath around neck and a sprig of celery in its mouth; skim and strain gravy; thicken with browned flour, boil up, add a glass of any good wine and juice of a lemon. Serve in a boat. In carving cut off head first; split down the back; take off hams and shoulders, and separate the ribs.

Roast Fillet of Veal.—Veal, ⅓ pint melted butter, ½ pound force-meat, 1 lemon. Bone the joint; make deep incision between fillet and saddle, and fill with force-meat. Bind joint in round form; fasten with skewers and twine; cover with buttered paper. Roast slowly at first. Baste well; take off paper just before done, dredge over a little flour, and baste with butter. Replace skewers with silver one. Pour over melted butter with juice of lemon and brown gravy. Garnish with sliced lemon. Time, 4 hours for 12 pounds.

Frogs.—Skin and dress the frogs, removing the head and feet; wipe dry with a towel; roll in seasoned cracker or bread crumbs. Fry in butter to a light brown.

Roast Lamb.—Lay in dripping-pan, dash cup cold water over it, and roast in oven; time, say, 10 minutes to pound. Baste often and freely, and after ½ hour cover with sheet buttered paper; 5 minutes before taking up, remove this, dredge with flour; as it browns bring to a froth with butter. Do not send gravy to table if you use mint sauce.

Mint Sauce.—2 tablespoonfuls green mint, chopped fine, 1 tablespoonful white sugar, 1 cup best cider vinegar. Put vinegar and sugar in sauce-boat and stir in mint; stand 15 minutes before serving.

To Give a Delicious Flavor to Lamb which is to be eaten cold, put in the water in which it is boiled whole cloves and long sticks of cinnamon. To one leg of lamb allow one small handful of cloves, and two or three sticks of cinnamon. If the lamb is to be roasted, boil the cloves and cinnamon in water, and baste the lamb with it.

Roast Venison or Mutton.—Take a leg of well-kept venison, wipe thoroughly, rub a little salt over it, dredge with flour. Place it in dripping-pan with ragged piece you have cut off, and a little water or wine. Put small bits of butter here and there over meat, set in oven and baste frequently until done. If leg is not very fat, it is a good plan to lard with strips of bacon or pork. Serve with currant jelly.

Ragout of Mutton.—3 lbs. mutton without bone; cut in strips 3 inches long by 1 inch wide; 2 lamb sweetbreads, 1 cup gravy made from bones, skin, etc.—"trimmings" of the meat—2 eggs, ¼ lb. salt pork, 1 fried onion, 1 cup green peas, pepper, salt and parsley, dripping for frying browned flour. Fry the onion in plenty of dripping, then the meat for 5 minutes; parboil the sweetbreads, throw into cold water to blanch, wipe and slice, then fry also in the fat. Lay sliced pork in the bottom of a saucepan, upon this the mutton, then the sweetbreads, next the onion, green peas, then pepper and salt, cover with gravy, put on a close lid, stew gently for 1 hour after the boil sets in. Take up the meat and sweetbreads, thicken gravy with browned flour, pour it on 2 beaten eggs, stir 1 minute over the fire, and pour upon the meat and serve

Sausages.—Have ¾ lean and ¼ fat pork, chopped very fine. 1 lb. salt, ¼ lb. pepper, and teacupful sage to every 40 lbs. meat. Warm the meat, that you can mix it well with your hands, do up a part in small patties with a little flour mixed with them, the rest pack in jars. When used, do it up in small cakes, flour the outside, fry in butter, or alone. They should not be covered while frying, or they will fall to pieces. They should be kept where it is cool, but not damp. To prevent sausages from bursting when cooking, never make a hole in them with a fork while turning them.

The "Fulton Market" Seasoning.—Is to 40 lbs. meat, 1 lb. salt, ¼ lb. pepper, ⅛ lb. powdered sage.

Smoked Venison.—Smoked venison is found in the markets during the spring months, good as smoked beef. Cut steaks, soak them in water, then broil as an ordinary steak; it can also be boiled like ham, but only requiring half the time. Smoked venison is usually tied up in canvas bags the same as Westphalia hams, and can be kept for a long time.

Stewed Squirrels.—3 fine gray squirrels, skinned and cleaned; joint as you would chicken for fricassee; ½ lb. fat salt pork, 1 onion (if liked) sliced, 12 ears corn cut from the cob 6 large tomatoes, pared and sliced, 3 tablespoonfuls butter, rolled in flour, parsley, enough water to cover squirrels. Put on squirrels, pork (cut up small), onion and parsley in the water and bring to boil. When this has lasted 10 minutes put in corn and stew until squirrels are tender. Then add the tomatoes, cut up thin, and 20 minutes later stir in butter and flour. Simmer 10 minutes, and serve in a large deep dish.

Stewed Rabbit.—2 rabbits, ½ pound fat salt pork, 1 large onion, 1 tablespoonful butter, 1 tablespoonful browned flour, pepper and salt, ½ lemon peeled and sliced thin, 1 glass sherry wine, ½ cup gravy. Slice the onion, dredge with flour and fry brown in the butter. Add ½ cupful gravy and when well mixed turn all into a saucepan. Put in the rabbits, jointed as for fricassee, the sliced bacon and lemon. Season, cover close and stew 1 hour, or until meat is tender. Thicken with browned flour, boil once and serve.

Stewed Beef Kidney.—Time, 30 minutes. A beef kidney; cut kidney into slices, season highly with pepper and salt, fry a light brown; then pour a little warm water into pan, dredge in some flour, put in slices of kidney; let them stew very gently. Sheep's kidneys should be split open, broiled over a clear fire, and served with a piece of butter placed on each half.

To Prepare Tripe for the table you should order it the day before you wish to serve it, scrape it thoroughly, wash it in several waters, then boil in salt and water until it is perfectly tender; let it drain in a platter all night. Next day cut it in small pieces and fry in hot lard after having rolled the pieces in flour. To serve with this make a rich, brown gravy, using a little of the lard in which the tripe was fried. If for breakfast, send baked potatoes, fried apples, and tomatoes with it; the tomatoes may be canned ones, cooked, and with thin slices of toasted bread put in the bottom of the dish.

Stew, Irish. — Time, about 2 hours. 2½ pounds of chops, 8 potatoes, 4 turnips, 4 small onions, nearly a quart of water. Take some chops from loin of mutton, place them in stewpan in alternate layers of sliced potatoes and chops; add turnips and onions cut into pieces, pour in nearly quart of cold water; cover stewpan closely, let it stew gently till vegetables are ready to mash and greater part of gravy is absorbed; then place in a dish; serve it up hot.

Souse. — Clean pig's feet and ears thoroughly, soak them a number of days in salt and water, boil tender and split them. They are good fried. To souse them cold, pour boiling vinegar over them, spiced with mace and pepper-corns. Cloves give them a dark color, but improve their taste. If a little salt be added, they will keep good, pickled, for month or two.

To Roast a Leg of Pork. — Choose a small leg of fine young pork; cut a slit in the knuckle with a sharp knife, and fill the space with sage and onions chopped, and a little pepper and salt. When half done score the skin in slices, but do not cut deeper than the outer rind. Apple sauce and potatoes should be served to eat with it.

Tripe Curry. — Boil 2 pounds of tripe and cut into strips; peel two large onions and cut them into square pieces, and put the onions into a stew-pan with three tablespoons butter. Let it stew till brown, stirring well, and mixing a tablespoonful curry powder. Now add 1 pint of milk and the cut up tripe. Let all stew for an hour skimming it well. Serve in a deep dish, with boiled rice, also, to eat with it. An East India curry powder is made thus: Pound very fine in a mortar 6 ounces coriander seed, ¾ ounce cayenne, 1½ ounces foenugreek seed, 1 ounce cumin seed, and 3 ounces turmeric. These articles can be bought at a druggist's. Pound fine, sift through fine muslin, spread on a dish and dry before the fire for 3 hours, stirring frequently. Keep this in a bottle with a glass stopper.

Tripe Fried. — Boil tripe tender and cut in pieces 3 or 4 inches square; make batter of 4 beaten eggs, 4 tablespoonfuls flour, and 1 pint of milk. Dip each piece of tripe in batter twice, lay in frying pan and fry brown. Serve hot.

Veal Cutlets. — Flatten with side of a hatchet. Pepper, salt, dip in raw egg, then in cracker dust; fry in a little butter, turning as they brown. Dish and pour over them some drawn butter in which has been cooked large spoonful tomato catsup.

Veal Chops with Tomato Sauce. — Trim and flatten the chops; dip in raw egg, then in cracker dust; fry slowly in lard or dripping; open can of tomatoes and drain off liquor. (Salt the rest of tomatoes and reserve for stewing or soup.) Put the liquor into saucepan with a sliced onion, and stew 10 minutes; strain out the onion, return juice to the fire, thicken with a large spoonful butter worked up in a teaspoonful corn-starch; pepper and salt, boil up quickly, and when you have laid chops upon a dish pour sauce over them and serve.

Veal Stew. — Cut 4 lbs. veal into strips 3 inches long and 1 inch thick, peel 12 large potatoes and cut into slices 1 inch thick, spread layer of veal on bottom of pot, sprinkle in a little salt and pepper, then layer of potatoes, then layer of veal seasoned as before. Use up veal thus: Over last layer of veal put layer of slices of salt pork, and over the whole, layer of potatoes. Pour in water till it rises an inch over the whole, cover close, heat 15 minutes and simmer an hour.

Sweetbreads. — Scald in salted water; remove stringy parts; put in cold water 5 or 10 minutes; drain in towel; dip in egg and bread or cracker crumbs, fry in butter, or boil them plain.

Veal Cutlets, Breaded. — Trim and flatten the cutlets, pepper and salt and roll in beaten egg, then in pounded cracker. Fry rather slowly in good dripping, turning when the lower side is brown. Drain off the fat, squeeze a little lemon juice upon each, and serve in a hot flat dish.

Stuffed Veal and Green Peas. — Take large bones from piece of loin of veal. Stuff the cavities thus made with a good force-meat of chopped pork, crumbs and seasoning. A few chopped mushrooms will improve it. Cover the sides with greased sheets of thick writing-paper. Put cupful soup stock or other gravy in the dripping-pan and baste well for 1 hour with butter and water, afterward with gravy. Cook fully 12 minutes to the pound. Take off paper during last ½ hour; dredge with flour, baste with butter, and brown nicely. Take up. Keep hot while you skim fat from gravy. Stir into it ½ cupful chopped mushrooms and a little browned flour. Have ready some green peas, boiled and seasoned, and make a circle of them about the veal when dished.

Veal Croquettes for breakfast can be prepared the night before, and so be ready for the table in a few minutes. Chop the veal fine; mix half a cup of sweet milk with about a teaspoonful of flour. Melt a piece of butter the size of an egg and stir the flour and milk in it; then let it come to a boil. Mix this thoroughly with the meat; form it in balls or flat cakes; lay on a platter; scatter a little pepper and salt over it, and let it stand until morning. Then beat one egg very light; add a little milk; dip the meat-balls in the egg, and then in cracker crumbs. Fry till brown in hot lard.

Rissolees of Veal. — Proceed as directed for *Chicken Rissolees,* substituting veal for chicken.

Rissolees of Beef. — Proceed as directed for *Chicken Rissolees,* substituting beef for chicken.

Eggs.

TO KEEP EGGS. — To 4 quarts air-slacked lime put 2 tablespoonfuls cream tartar, 2 of salt, and 4 quarts cold water. Put fresh eggs into stone jar, pour this mixture over them. This will keep 9 dozen; if fresh when laid down, they will keep many months. If water settles away, so as to leave upper layer uncovered, add more water. Cover close, keep in cool place.

Eggs Poached. — Nearly fill frying-pan with boiling water; add a little salt and vinegar. Break eggs one at a time into wet saucer; slip from this upon surface of water. Cook slowly 3 minutes; take up with perforated skimmer; lay carefully upon buttered toast.

Relishes.

GOLDEN BUCK. — A "Golden Buck" is merely the addition of a poached egg, which is put carefully on top of rarebit.

Made Mustard. — 4 tablespoonfuls English mustard, 2 teaspoonfuls salt, 2 teaspoonfuls white sugar, 2 teaspoonfuls salad oil, 1 teaspoonful pepper, vinegar to make smooth paste — that from celery or onion pickle is best. Rub mustard, oil, sugar, pepper and salt together. Wet by degrees with vinegar, beating very hard at the last, when proper consistency has been gained. Will be found far superior to mustard usually mixed for the table.

Welsh Rarebit. — Select richest and best American cheese, the milder the better, as melting brings out strength. To make 5 rarebits, take 1 pound cheese, grate and put in tin or porcelain-lined saucepan; add ale (old is best) enough to thin the cheese sufficiently, say about a wineglassful to each rarebit. Place over fire, stir until it is melted. Have slice of toast ready for each rarebit (crusts trimmed); put a slice on each plate, and pour cheese enough over each piece to cover it. Serve while hot.

Yorkshire Rarebit. — Same as "Golden Buck," only it has 2 thin slices of broiled bacon on top.

Poultry.

TO ROAST A FOWL.—Time, 1 hour. 1 large fowl, 2 or 3 large spoonfuls bread crumbs, pepper and salt, ½ lb. butter. Prepare fowl for roasting; put into inside bread crumbs, seasoned with pepper, salt and piece of butter size of large walnut. Roast at a clear fire, basting well with butter; just before done, dredge with flour, and baste again with butter. When done, add little warm water to butter in dripping-pan, or a little *very thin* melted butter, and strain over fowl. Serve with bread sauce, or little gravy in tureen if preferred.

Roast Chicken.—Singe and truss carefully. Broilers, as they are called, are better without stuffing, unless very large. Season with salt, put small bits of butter over meat and place in pan with a little water; baste occasionally and dredge with flour before taking from oven. A spring chicken cooked in any style is not to be despised. But a well-known epicure once said:

"To roast spring chicken is to spoil it. Just split it down the back and broil it."

Goose.—This requires keeping, the same as fowls, some days before cooking. The goose is best in the autumn and early part of winter—never good in spring. What is called a green goose is four months old. It is insipid after that, though tender. Pick well and singe the goose, then clean carefully. Put the liver and gizzard on to cook as a turkey's. When the goose is washed, and ready for stuffing, have boiled three white potatoes, skin and mash them; chop three onions very fine, throw them into cold water; stir into the potatoes a spoonful of butter, a little salt and black pepper, a tablespoonful of finely-rubbed sage leaves; drain off the onions and mix with the potato, sage, etc. When well mixed, stuff the goose with the mixture. Have ready a coarse needle and thread, and sew up the slit made for cleaning and introducing the stuffing. A full-grown goose requires 1¾ hours. Roast it as a turkey, dredging and basting. The gravy is prepared as for poultry, with the liver and gizzard. Apple-sauce is indispensable for roast goose.

Roast Goose or Duck. Singe, draw, and truss fowl; if an old one parboil it; best stuffing for a goose is sage and onions. If a strong flavor of onions is liked, they should be chopped raw. If this is not the case, should be boiled in 1 or 2 waters, and mixed with bread crumbs powdered sage, salt, pepper, and Royal Extract *Nutmeg* to taste. Fill bird with stuffing, sew up with coarse thread, sprinkle salt over, and set in pan with a little warm water. Baste frequently, and do not take from oven until thoroughly cooked.

Apple Sauce.—Pare, core, and slice tart apples, stew in water enough to cover them until they break to pieces. Beat to a pulp with a good lump of butter and plenty of sugar; serve cold.

To Bake a Turkey.—Let the turkey be picked, singed and washed, and wiped dry, inside and out; joint only to the first joint in the legs, and cut some of the neck off if it is all bloody; then cut 1 dozen small gashes in the fleshy parts of the turkey—on the outside and in different parts—and press 1 whole oyster in each gash, then close the skin and flesh over each gash as tight'y as possible; then stuff your turkey, leaving a little room for the stuffing to swell. When stuffed, sew it up with a stout cord, rub over lightly with flour, sprinkle a little salt and pepper on it, and put some in your dripping-pan; put in your turkey, baste it often with its own drippings; bake to a nice brown; thicken your gravy with a little flour and water. Be sure and keep the bottom of the dripping-pan covered with water or it will burn the gravy and make it bitter.

Stewed Cranberries.—Wash and look over carefully. Place in saucepan, little more than covered with water. Cover saucepan and stew until skins are tender, adding more water if necessary; add 1 pound sugar to each pound of berries. Let them simmer 10 or 12 minutes, then set away in a bowl or wide-mouthed crock.

To Truss and Roast a Partridge or Pheasant.—Time, 25 to 30 minutes. Partridges should hang a few days. Pluck, draw and wipe partridge; cut off head, leaving sufficient skin on neck to skewer back; bring legs close to breast, between it and side bones, pass skewer through pinions and thick part of thighs. Roast and serve with a little gravy poured over birds, and bread-sauce and gravy in tureens.

Fried Spring Chicken.—Clean and joint, then soak in salt-water for 2 hours. Put in frying-pan equal parts of lard and butter—in all enough to cover chicken. Roll each piece in flour, or dip in beaten egg, then roll in cracker crumbs, and drop into the boiling fat. Fry until browned on both sides. Serve on flat platter garnished with sprigs of parsley. Pour most of fat from frying-pan, thicken the remainder with browned flour, add to it cup of boiling water or milk. Serve in gravy-boat.

Fricasseed Chickens.—Clean, wash and joint the fowls, lay in cold salt and water for an hour. Put in pot with ½ lb. salt pork, cut in strips, and cold water enough to cover them. Cover close and heat slowly to a gentle boil; when fowls are full size and fairly tender, stew 1 hour or more after they begin to boil. When done add half-chopped onions, parsley and pepper, cover again for ten minutes. Stir up two tablespoonfuls flour in cold water, then into a cup of hot milk, and this in turn into 2 beaten eggs, then put in 1 large spoonful butter, and pour all into the saucepan; mix well, boil fairly, place chickens on your dish and pour the gravy over them and serve.

Chicken Patés.—Chop meat of cold chicken fine and season well. Make large cupful rich drawn butter, and while on fire stir in 2 eggs, boiled hard, minced very fine, also a little chopped parsley, then chicken meat. Let almost boil. Have ready some paté-pans of good paste, baked quickly to light brown. Slip from pans while hot, fill with mixture and set in oven to heat. Arrange upon dish and serve hot.

Chicken Pie.—Take 2 full-grown chickens, or more if small, disjoint them, cut backbone, etc., small as convenient. Boil them with few slices of salt pork in water enough to cover them, let boil quite tender, then take out breast bone. After they boil, and scum is taken off, put in a little onion cut very fine—not enough to taste distinctly, just enough to flavor a little; rub some parsley very fine when dry, or cut fine when green—this gives pleasant flavor. Season well with pepper and salt, and few ounces good fresh butter. When all is cooked well, have liquid enough to cover chicken, then beat 2 eggs and stir in some sweet cream. Line 5-quart pan with crust made like soda biscuit, only more shortening, put in chicken and liquid, cover with crust same as lining. Bake till crust is done, and you will have a good chicken pie.

Chicken Pie, a la Reine.—Paste No. 3; 1 plump, tender chicken, ½ pound salt pork, ½ teaspoonful each Royal celery, salt and thyme, 4 sprigs parsley, white pepper and salt to taste. Cut chicken up in small joints, the pork in neat scallops, stew gently in 1½ pints water, until nearly cooked. Line edge of pudding dish with the paste, make layers of chicken, pork and seasonings, when used, sprinkle over the chopped parsley; fill with the gravy, cover, ornament, and wash over with milk; bake in steady oven 40 minutes.

Boned Chicken.—Boil a chicken in little water as possible until meat will fall from bones; remove all skin, chop together light and dark parts; season with pepper and salt. Boil down liquid in which chicken was boiled, then pour it on meat; place in tin, wrap tightly in cloth, press with heavy weight several hours. When served, cut in thin slices.

Chicken Pie. — 2 chickens, jointed small ; cook tender, season with butter, salt and pepper ; thicken gravy with flour. Make crust as for soda biscuit ; line sides of pie dish with crust ½ inch thick ; fill dish with chicken and gravy ; cover with crust ; bake ½ hour.

Chicken Pot-pie. — 2 large chickens jointed and boiled in 2 quarts water ; add a few slices salt pork ; season. When nearly cooked, add crust made of 1 quart flour, 4 teaspoonfuls Royal Baking Powder 1 saltspoonful salt ; stir in stiff batter with water ; drop into kettle while boiling ; cover close and cook 25 minutes.

Rissolees of Chicken. — *Pie Paste No. 1* (*Chromsky Mixture*). Roll out the paste very thin, cut out with large biscuit cutter, wet the edges, put a teaspoonful of the mixture, fold the paste over it, pressing the two edges. Fry in plenty of lard, made hot for the purpose, until the paste is cooked. Serve on a napkin.

Chicken Fritters. — Cold chicken, salt and pepper, lemon juice, batter. Cut the cold chicken in small pieces, put in a dish, season with salt, pepper and juice of a lemon. Let this stand 1 hour. Then make a batter of 2 eggs to a pint of milk, a little salt, and flour enough to make a batter not too stiff. Stir the chicken in this, and drop it by spoonfuls in boiling fat. Fry brown, drain and serve. Any kind of tender cold meat can be used in this way.

Chicken a l'Italienne. — *Common Batter*, remains of chicken, 12 tomatoes, 1 cup broth, 2 tablespoonfuls onion chopped, 1 tablespoonful parsley, 1 saltspoonful each salt, white pepper, Royal thyme, and summer savory, 1 tablespoonful butter. Cut remains of chicken into small pieces ; dip into batter, and fry crisp in plenty of lard made hot for the purpose ; serve with *Tomato Sauce.*

Stewed Chicken. — Prepare and cook chicken in same manner as for chicken pie ; just before chicken is quite done pare quantity of potatoes, cut them in two lay them on top of chicken, let them boil until done ; then take potatoes up on plate by themselves, turn pint of sweet cream in with chicken, thicken with flour, wet with sweet milk, season with pepper, salt, and plenty of butter. Sweet milk will answer in place of cream, but will require more butter.

Turkey Hash and Poached Eggs. — Cold fowl may be turned into hot breakfast dish as follows : Chop meat very fine, put ½ pint gravy into stew-pan with little piece of butter rolled in flour, teaspoonful catsup, some pepper and salt, and peel of ½ lemon, shred very fine ; put in turkey or chicken, and shake over clear fire till thoroughly hot. Above proportions are for cold turkey. It may be served with 2 or more poached eggs. If there are not eggs enough to allow one for each guest, they should be broken with spoon and mixed with hash just before serving. Serve hot.

Dressing for Turkey or Roast Meats. — Mix stale bread crumbs or pounded cracker with butter, salt, pepper and an egg ; add Royal summer savory or Royal sage ; if desired, oysters chopped may be added. Mix thoroughly together, adding a little warm water for wetting if necessary.

Toast.

ZWIEBACK. — ½ pound flour, ½ pint milk, 2 eggs, ½ pound butter, 3 heaping teaspoonfuls Royal Baking Powder, ½ teacupful sugar, and 1 teaspoonful salt. Sift together flour and baking powder. Rub in the butter, sugar and salt, adding the eggs 1 at a time ; then add milk and flour gradually, making a nice batter — not too stiff ; pour into well buttered, low cake pan, bake in moderate oven about ½ hour. When done, take carefully out of pan and let cool. On the following day cut with sharp knife into slices about ½ inch thick, and toast in moderate oven.

Graham Cream Toast. — Cut 6 slices delicate Graham bread, 1 pint rich cream, butter, salt, to taste. Toast bread brown, scrape off the burnt, if any, remove crust, butter, cut in 4 pieces ; arrange them in suitable dish with cover, bring the cream to boil, with pinch of salt, pour over toast, cover and serve.

Canapees au Fromage (Fried Bread with melted Cheese). — 4 lunch rolls, 2 ounces butter, 4 ounces rich cheese. Remove from rolls the tops and bottoms, very thin, cut in 2 slices, fry them yellow in butter ; lay cheese cut in thin slices, one on each canapée. Set in oven a moment to melt cheese. Serve at once.

Poached Eggs on Toast. — 4 slices, cut thin, of unfermented Graham bread, butter, salt, vinegar, 8 eggs, parsley. Toast bread delicately, cut off crust, divide half, and butter. Meanwhile have a shallow stewpan ¾ full of water, large pinch salt, 1 teaspoonful vinegar, and 2 sprigs parsley tied in a bouquet ; when water boils drop in eggs, 1 at a time ; at once set stewpan where it will not boil. Allow eggs to simmer 2 minutes, gently take them up with skimmer, lay each one on piece of toast. Serve garnished with lettuce leaves.

Anchovy Toast. — 4 lunch rolls, butter, 6 anchovies, ½ pint cream, 3 egg yelks, salt. Remove tops and bottoms from rolls, very thin, cut in 2 slices, toast and butter them. Wash and remove bones from anchovies, chop exceedingly fine, spread on 4 of the pieces of toast ; cover with remainder, arrange on their dish, and pour over custard prepared from cream and egg yelks in following manner : Place cream and little salt in small tin, which put in saucepan containing boiling water ; soon as cream comes to boiling point stir in yelks, which have been beaten with a little cream. Place over fire until it thickens, and use as directed.

Ham Toast. — 3 Graham muffins, butter, 6 ounces of ham, 2 anchovies, pinch of cayenne. Cut each muffin into 3 slices, toast brown and butter ; chop ham, pound it with cayenne and anchovies washed, free of bones and skin ; use it equally spread on toast ; lay on tin, with small piece of butter on each ; set in not very hot oven to gently warm through ; serve at once, either for breakfast, lunch or supper.

Sauces and Dressings for Meats.

BREAD SAUCE. — Quarter and boil 1 large onion with some black peppers and milk, till onion is quite a pulp. Pour milk strained on grated white stale bread, and cover it. In an hour put it into saucepan, with a good piece of butter mixed with a little flour ; boil the whole up together and serve.

Bread Sauce for Partridges or Grouse. — 1 cup of stale bread crumbs, 1 onion, 2 ozs, butter, pepper and salt, a little mace. Cut the onion fine and boil it in milk till quite soft ; then strain the milk on to the stale bread crumbs, and let it stand an hour. Put it in a saucepan with the boiled onion, pepper, salt and mace. Give it a boil, and serve in sauce tureen. This sauce can also be used for grouse, and is very nice. Roast partridges are nice served with bread crumbs, fried brown in butter, with cranberry or currant jelly laid beside them in the platter.

Caper Sauce. — 2 tablespoonfuls butter, 1 tablespoonful flour ; mix well ; pour on boiling water till it thickens ; add one hard-boiled egg chopped fine, and 2 tablespoonfuls capers.

Drawn Butter. — ½ a cup butter, 2 tablespoonfuls flour ; rubbed thoroughly together, then stir into pint boiling water ; little salt ; parsley if wished.

Celery, Mayonnaise. — Yelk of 1 egg, a pinch of mustard, a little salt, very little pepper, juice of ½ lemon and some water. Beat all together, pour 4 ounces olive oil in drop by drop, then add small spoonful of boiling water to mayonnaise. Take 6 heads of well-washed celery, wipe with towel, and cut them in pieces in salad bowl. Throw the mayonnaise over celery ; mix all together, and serve. (Can curl celery by twisting each branch round a skewer and throwing it in cold water.)

Egg Sauce. — 1 cup of chicken broth, heated and thickened, with tablespoonful of butter rolled thickly in flour, poured over 2 beaten eggs ; boiled 1 minute, with tablespoonful parsley stirred in ; then seasoned and poured upon pounded yelks of 2 boiled eggs placed in bottom of bowl. Stir up and it is ready.

Gravy for Roast Meats. — After taking out meat, pour off fat ; add water, season, and thicken with flour.

Gravy for Turkey. — Boil giblets very tender: chop fine ; then take liquor in which they are boiled, thicken with flour ; season with salt, pepper, and a little butter; add giblets, and dripping in which turkey was roasted.

Horse-radish Sauce. — 1 dessert spoonful of olive oil, same quantity of powdered mustard. 1 tablespoonful of vinegar, 2 of grated horse-radish and 1 teaspoonful of salt.

Mayonnaise Sauce. — Work yelks of 2 raw eggs to a smooth paste, add 2 saltspoonfuls salt, ½ saltspoonful cayenne pepper, saltspoonful dry mustard, and teaspoonful salad oil. Mix these ingredients thoroughly and add strained juice of ½ a lemon. Take remainder of ½ pint finest salad oil and add gradually teaspoonful at a time. Every fifth teaspoonful add few drops of lemon juice, until you have used 2 lemons and ½ pint of oil. There are almost as many ways of making mayonnaise sauce as there are of cooking eggs.

Mint Sauce. — Mix 1 tablespoonful white sugar to ½ teacupful good vinegar; add mint chopped fine; ½ teaspoonful salt. Serve with roast lamb or mutton.

Oyster Sauce. — 1 pint oysters, ½ lemon, 2 tablespoonfuls butter rolled well in flour, 1 teacup milk, cayenne pepper and nutmeg to taste. Heat the oyster liquor and when it boils skim, and put in oysters. Soon as they boil stir in butter, cut up and well floured, spice and lemon juice. Boil 5 minutes ; take from fire and put with milk which has been heated in another vessel. Stir up well and serve.

Onion Sauce. — Time, nearly ½ an hour. 4 or 5 white onions, ½ pint hot milk, 1 oz, butter, pepper and salt to taste. Peel onions and boil till tender, press water from them, chop them very fine, make milk hot, pulp onions with it; add butter, pepper and salt to taste.

To Make Sage and Onion Dressing, for Roast Pig or Roast Pork. Time 25 to 30 minutes. 2 large onions, double the quantity bread crumbs, 3 teaspoonfuls chopped sage, 2 oz. butter, 1 egg, pepper and salt. Boil onions in 2 or 3 waters, to take off strong taste in them ; then drain them, chop up fine, mix with bread crumbs, minced sage, butter, pepper and salt; mix the whole with well-beaten yelk of an egg to bind it.

Salad Dressing. — Beat 4 eggs light, add 1 tablespoonful mixed mustard, ½ teaspoonful salt. 5 tablespoonfuls vinegar, a little cayenne pepper: mix well, then stand in dish filled with boiling water ; when warmed through add tablespoonful butter; cook until little thicker than custard, stirring constantly. If desired it may be boiled until thicker, then thinned with milk or cream.

To Prepare Curry Powder. — 1 ounce ginger, 1 ounce mustard, 1 ounce pepper, 3 of coriander seed, 3 of turmeric, ¼ an ounce cardamons, ¼ ounce cayenne pepper, ¼ ounce cinnamon, and ¼ ounce cumin seed. Pound fine, sift, and cork tight in bottle.

Oyster Dressing. — 2 tablespoonfuls flour, 2 tablespoonfuls butter; brown butter and flour in dripper: add water to make thin for gravy; boil; add 1 pint oysters chopped ; pepper and salt to taste.

Sauce Piquante. — 1 cupful liquor from tongue or any other kind of meat, 2 tablespoonfuls butter. 1 teaspoonful fresh made mustard, a little salt and pepper, 1 heaping tablespoonful browned flour, 1 teaspoonful mixed parsley and sweet marjoram, 1 tablespoonful onion vinegar. Brown butter by shaking it over a clear fire in saucepan. Heat cupful liquor to a boil, skim and season with salt and pepper, skim again before stirring in flour, wet up with cold water ; as it thickens put in batter, herbs, mustard and vinegar. Boil up ; pour half over tongue, the rest into sauce bowl.

Sauce for Boiled Cod, and other kinds of Fish. — To 1 gill boiling water add as much milk; stir into this while boiling 2 tablespoonfuls butter gradually, 1 tablespoonful flour wet up with cold water ; as it thickens, the chopped yelk 1 boiled egg and one raw egg beaten light. Take directly from fire, season with pepper, salt, a little chopped parsley and juice one lemon, and set covered in boiling water (but not over fire) 5 minutes, stirring occasionally. Pour part of sauce over fish when dished ; the rest in a boat. Serve mashed potatoes with it.

Sauce for Salmon, and other Fish. — 1 cupful milk heated to a boil and thickened with tablespoonful corn starch previously wet up with cold water, the liquor from the salmon. 1 gravy spoonful butter, 1 raw egg beaten light, juice ½ lemon, mace and cayenne pepper to taste. Add the egg to thickened milk when you have stirred in butter and liquor; take from fire, season and let stand in hot water 3 minutes, covered. Lastly put in lemon juice and turn out immediately. Pour it all over and around the salmon.

Sauce for Wild Ducks, Teal, etc. — Take proper quantity of veal gravy, pepper and salt to taste ; squeeze in the juice of 2 good oranges, add a little red wine ; let wine boil some time in the gravy.

Shrimp Sauce. — Wash clean ½ pint of shrimps, put them in stewpan with 1 spoonful anchovy liquor, and ½ pound thick melted butter. Boil up for 5 minutes and squeeze in ½ lemon. Toss it up and pour into sauce boat.

Sauce (Italian). — Put a lump fresh butter into stewpan with some mushrooms, onions, parsley, and ½ laurel leaf, all cut fine ; set over the fire for some time and shake in a little flour ; moisten it with a glass white wine, and as much good broth, adding salt, pepper, and a little mace beaten fine ; boil ½ hour ; skim off the fat and serve. Can give a fine flavor by putting in a bunch sweet herbs while boiling ; take them out before serving the sauce.

Sauce for Venison. — 2 spoonfuls currant jelly, 1 stick cinnamon, 1 blade mace, grated white bread, 10 tablespoonfuls water; let stew with little water ; serve in dish with venison steak.

Tomato Sauce. — Pare, slice and stew tomatoes for 20 minutes, strain and rub through a sieve, leaving hard and tough parts behind. Put into saucepan with a little minced onion, parsley, pepper, salt and sugar. Bring to boil ; stir in good spoonful butter rolled in flour. Boil up and serve.

Tomato Sauce. — Place on fire tomatoes washed, broth, onion, parsley, and seasonings. Boil to pulp — about 35 minutes ; rub through fine sieve, return to fire, make it hot, stir in batter, and serve.

Yorkshire Pudding. ¾ pint flour, 3 eggs. 1½ pints milk, pinch salt, 1½ teaspoonfuls Royal Baking Powder. Sift flour and powder together, add eggs, beaten with milk, stir quickly into rather thinner batter than for griddle cake, pour into dripping pan, plentifully spread with fresh cold beef drippings, bake in hot oven 25 minutes ; serve with roast beef.

Salads.

CABBAGE SALAD.—Chop the cabbage fine, sprinkle with salt, and let stand over night; beat one egg thoroughly, and add to ⅓ pint boiling vinegar; rub 2 tablespoonfuls mustard into more vinegar to form a smooth paste; add this to the boiling vinegar; pepper and sugar to taste. Let all come to boil, and pour over the cabbage, stirring thoroughly.

Celery Salad.—2 bunches celery, 1 tablespoonful salad oil; 4 tablespoonfuls vinegar; 1 small teaspoonful fine sugar; pepper and salt to taste. Wash and scrape celery; lay in ice cold water until dinner time. Then cut into inch lengths, add above seasoning. Stir well together with fork and serve in salad bowl.

Chicken Salad.—Cut meat from your cold chicken; add equal quantity of shred lettuce; when you have cut chicken into narrow strips 2 inches long, mix in bowl, and prepare following dressing: Beat yelks of 2 eggs, salt lightly, and beat in, few drops at a time, 4 tablespoonfuls salad oil; then, as gradually, 3 teaspoonfuls of Royal Extract Celery. The mixture should be thick as cream. Pour over meat and lettuce. Stir up with fork (silver fork if you have it); place salad in glass dish.

Lobster Salad.—Tear meat of lobster into shreds with two forks; remove eggs (if hen lobster) from fins; scrape out all green fat from shell and set aside. Prepare for making a mayonnaise by working tablespoonful of fat with yelk of 1 raw egg, and 1 hard boiled egg. Let this be basis of your mayonnaise; in all other particulars follow instructions for mayonnaise sauce. When complete, mix lobster meat with 3 tablespoonfuls sauce. Cover bottom of dish with lettuce (the large leaves tear in two); put layer of lobster upon it. Next add layer of celery cut into narrow strips, and another layer of lobster; arrange neatly on dish; sprinkle eggs or chopped coral on lettuce round the edges; pour sauce over meat, garnish with lobster legs, and serve.

Tomato Salad.—Pare with sharp knife. Slice and lay in salad bowl. Make dressing as follows: Work up saltspoonful each of salt, pepper, and fresh made mustard, with two tablespoonfuls of salad oil, adding only a few drops at a time, and, when thoroughly mixed, whip in with an egg beaten 4 tablespoonfuls of vinegar; toss up with fork.

Cucumber and Onion Salad.—Pare cucumbers and lay in ice-water 1 hour; do same with onions in another bowl. Then slice them in proportion of 1 onion to 3 large cucumbers; arrange in salad bowl, and season with vinegar, pepper and salt.

Lettuce Salad.—Use ⅓ as much salad oil as you do vinegar; pepper and salt to suit taste. Cut up young lettuce with sharp knife, pile in salad bowl; sprinkle with powdered sugar, pour rest of ingredients, mixed together, over salad. Stir up with fork to mix well.

Oyster Salad.—Cut oysters into thirds or quarters. Pull hearts out of nice lettuce heads and shred up ⅓ as much as you have oysters. Dressing to be made in following proportions: 2 tablespoonfuls salad oil to 4 of vinegar, 1 teaspoonful salt and same of sugar, ½ teaspoonful each pepper and fresh made mustard. Rub up, mix thoroughly, and pour over oysters and lettuce just before serving.

Potato Salad.—Slice ½ dozen large cold, boiled potatoes; put into salad dish and season as follows: 2 tablespoonfuls best salad oil; add ½ teaspoonful sugar, same of pepper, made mustard, and salt, and about same of Royal celery salt added improves salad greatly. Rub to smooth paste, and whip in teaspoonful at a time, 5 tablespoonfuls best vinegar. When thoroughly mixed pour upon salad and serve.

Lettuce Salad, With Cream Dressing.—¼ cup new milk (cream is best), 1 teaspoon corn starch, whites 2 eggs beaten stiff, 3 tablespoonfuls vinegar, 2 tablespoonfuls best salad oil, 2 teaspoonfuls powdered sugar, 1 teaspoonful salt, ½ teaspoonful pepper, 1 teaspoonful fresh made mustard. Heat milk (or cream) almost to boiling; stir in corn starch wet up with cold milk. Then boil up, add sugar and take from fire. Cool; beat in frothed whites, oil, pepper, mustard and salt; when lettuce is shred fine, add vinegar to dressing and pour over it. Stir up with a fork and serve.

Omelettes.

OMELETTE.—Soak teacup bread crumbs in cup sweet milk over night, 3 eggs, beat yelks and whites separately; mix yelks with the bread and milk; stir in whites, add teaspoonful salt, fry brown. This is sufficient for 6 persons.

Baked Omelette.—4 or 6 eggs; beat whites separately; small teacup milk, butter size of walnut; 1 tablespoonful flour, a little salt. Beat yelks, add butter, milk, flour and salt, lastly the beaten whites. Butter a dish just the size to hold it; bake in quick oven.

Omelette Souffle.—Break 6 eggs into separate cups; beat 4 of the yelks, mix with them teaspoonful of flour, 3 tablespoonfuls of powdered sugar. Very little salt, flavor with Royal Extract Lemon or any other of the Royal flavors that may be preferred. Whisk the whites of the 6 eggs to firm froth; mix them lightly with yelks; pour the mixture into a greased pan or dish; bake in quick oven. When well risen and lightly browned on the top it is done; roll out in dish, sift pulverized sugar over and send to table. You can also pour some rum over it and set it on fire as for an omelette au rhum.

Oyster Omelette.—Stew 6 oysters in their own liquor; remove oysters and thicken liquid with butter rolled in flour; season with salt, cayenne pepper, mix with it teaspoonful chopped parsley. Chop up oysters and add them to sauce; simmer gently until same thickens. Beat 3 eggs lightly with 1½ tablespoonfuls of cream, fry until they are delicately set; before folding over put a few spoonfuls of mixture in center; turn it carefully on a hot dish, with balance of sauce around it. Serve immediately. If small oysters are used put them in center of omelette, whole; fold and serve with sauce around it.

Kidney Omelette.—Made same as Ham, except the kidney is first stewed. Beef kidney chopped very fine, same as mince-meat; put in stewpan and pepper and salt to taste. Stew for ½ hour or more. When done pour off juice. Beat together whites and yelks of 12 eggs. Stir kidney in the eggs; add lump of butter size of an egg; place again on fire, when done serve hot. Above makes two omelettes.

Tomato Omelette.—Skin 2 or 3 tomatoes; cut in slices; fry in butter; beat up some eggs to make omelette; season with salt and pepper; warm some butter in pan; put in eggs, stirring well to keep from adhering; mix in tomatoes, turn out omelette on plate, doubling it in two. Another nice way is to roll up tomatoes in omelette, and serve with tomato sauce.

Ham Omelette.—3 pounds ham well broiled and chopped very fine (like mince-meat), 7 eggs, 4 tablespoonfuls milk, pepper and a little salt, 1 large spoonful of butter; beat together the eggs (white and yelks) with a few whirls of the beater; put in the milk and beat fast 1 minute; stir the ham in the eggs; then pour into a frying-pan in which the butter is heating, not hissing; shake briskly over the fire, slipping cake turner under it to prevent sticking, and in 4 minutes double it over in the middle, and turn it out into a hot dish by a dexterous inversion of the pan, and serve.

French Omelette. — Take 4 eggs, separate the yelks from the whites. Beat the whites to a snow on a dinner plate; then beat the yelks in small basin, with sugar to taste; then add a small pinch of Royal Baking Powder, and 3 large tablespoonfuls of flour, and milk enough to make a thin batter. Then pour into an omelette pan, previously heated and greased. Spread the white over the top. Fry by holding high above the fire till set brown on the top; double over and serve hot with jam.

Vegetables.

HINTS ON COOKING VEGETABLES. First—Have them fresh as possible. Summer vegetables should be cooked on same day they are gathered. Second—Look them over and wash well, cutting out all decayed or unripe parts. Third—Lay them, when peeled, in cold water for some time before using. Fourth—Always let water boil before putting them in, and continue to boil until done.
Turnips—Should be peeled, and boiled from 40 minutes to an hour.
Beets—Boil from 1 to 2 hours; then put in cold water and slip skin off.
Spinach—Boil 20 minutes.
Parsnips—Boil from 20 to 30 minutes.
Onions—Best boiled in two or three waters; adding milk the last time.
String Beans—Should be boiled 1 hour.
Shell Beans—Require ½ hour to an hour.
Green Corn—Boil 20 or 30 minutes.
Green Peas—Should be boiled in little water as possible; boil 20 minutes.
Asparagus—Same as peas; serve on toast with cream gravy.
Winter Squash—Cut in pieces and boil 20 to 40 minutes in small quantity of water; when done, press water out, mash smooth, season with butter, pepper and salt.
Cabbage—Should be boiled from ½ hour to 1 hour in plenty of water; salt while boiling.

Asparagus on Toast. Cut stalks of equal length, rejecting woody portions, and scrapings, the whiter parts retained. Tie in bunch with soft tape and cook about 30 minutes, if of fair size; if small, 20 minutes. Have ready 6 or 8 slices nicely toasted bread. Dip in asparagus liquor, butter well and lay on hot dish. Drain the asparagus; untie, and arrange on toast. Pepper and salt to taste.

Celery. — Wash, scrape, trim off green tops, and throw aside for seasoning soups, vinegar, etc., the rank green stalks. Lay better parts in cold water until wanted for table. Put into celery boat.

Baked Beans. — 1 quart beans soaked over night; in morning put them in kettle with cold water and boil 10 minutes; change water and put with them small piece of salt pork. Let boil until nearly tender, then take out of kettle with skimmer, put in baking dish with pork in center; cut rind in small squares; sprinkle over the top 1 tablespoonful white sugar; bake 3 hours. If they bake dry, add bean broth.

Boston Baked Beans No. 2. — A quart of white beans, covered with 2 quarts lukewarm water in a tin pan, should be placed on back of range early in the morning, say 8 o'clock. At noon, if the heat has been sufficient, they will have a shriveled appearance and be slightly soft to pressure. Now have ready an earthen bean-pot which comes for the purpose, with a pound of salt pork, uncooked, in the bottom, which is to be covered with beans; add pepper, no salt, as the pork is sufficiently salt, and about 1 large tablespoonful of New Orleans molasses, to give fine color, then fill up with water and set in moderate oven to bake slowly 6 hours, occasionally adding water if necessary, to keep moist.

Lima Beans. — Put a pint of select beans in boiling salted water enough to cover. Cook until tender, then drain them. Melt a piece of butter the size of an egg, and mix an even teaspoonful of flour with it. Add a little meat broth to make a smooth sauce, or use water instead. Put the beans in the sauce and set them at the side of the fire for 15 minutes. Just before serving add a tablespoonful of chopped parsley, and season to taste with salt and pepper.

To Boil Asparagus. — 1 tablespoonful of salt to ½ gallon of water. Scrape clean all the white parts of the stalks from the asparagus, and throw them into cold water; tie them up in bundles, cut the root ends even, and put them in a piece of muslin to preserve the tops. Have ready a wide stewpan, with the salt and water boiling; lay in the asparagus, and boil it quickly until it is tender. Have a thin slice of toasted bread, cut in square pieces, laid at the bottom of the dish. Take up the asparagus, lay it on the toast with the white ends upwards, and the points meeting in the center. Serve with butter. Time, 15 to 18 minutes after the water boils.

Baked Squash. — Boil, mash, and let get cold; then beat up light with 1 tablespoonful melted butter, 2 raw eggs, 3 tablespoonfuls milk, pepper and salt to taste. Put in buttered bake dish, sift dry crumbs over the top, and bake in a quick oven.

Buttered Parsnips. — Boil tender and scrape; slice lengthwise. Put 3 tablespoonfuls butter in a saucepan, with pepper, salt, and a little chopped parsley. When heated put in the parsnips. Shake and turn until mixture boils, then lay the parsnips in order upon a dish, and pour the butter over them and serve.

To Boil Parsnips. — 1 large spoonful of salt to 1½ gallon of water. If parsnips are young they require only to be scraped before boiling; old ones must be pared thin and cut into quarters. Put them into a stewpan of boiling salt and water. Boil them quickly until tender, take them up, drain them, and serve them on a vegetable dish. Time, 1 hour to 1½ hours; if small, ½ hour to 1 hour.

Baked Macaroni. — Break ½ pound macaroni in pieces an inch long, cook in boiling water, slightly salted, 20 minutes. Drain, and put a layer in bottom of a greased bake dish, upon this some grated cheese and tiny bits of butter; then more macaroni, and so on, filling dish, with grated cheese on top. Wet with a little milk and salt lightly. Cover and bake ½ hour; brown, and serve in a bake dish.

Boiled Artichokes. — Soak artichokes, wash them in several waters; cut stalks even, trim away lower leaves and ends of the others; boil in salted water with tops downwards; let them remain until leaves can be easily drawn out. Before serving remove the choke and serve with melted butter.

To Boil Jerusalem Artichokes. — To each gallon of water, 2 large spoonfuls of salt. Wash artichokes, peel or cut them into a round or oval form, and put them into a large saucepan of cold water, with salt in the above proportion. They will take 20 minutes from the time the water boils to become tender. When done, drain them, and serve them with a little melted butter poured over them. Time, 20 minutes.

Cauliflower. — Plunge a head of cauliflower in salt-water several times to remove any insect. Boil 10 minutes in salt-water, drain on sieve, put cauliflower in buttered dish. Melt piece of butter size of an egg; add to it 1 tablespoonful flour, stir on the fire 1 minute; add gill of milk, a quantity of grated cheese, pepper and salt. Stir this sauce till it boils. Pour over the cauliflower, sprinkle over it a few browned bread crumbs, set it in moderate oven for a few minutes to bake.

Fried Onions. — Peel (holding onions and hands under water to prevent tears), wash and cut crosswise so as to form undivided rings. Flour them, fry 5 or 6 minutes. Drain, sprinkle with salt and pepper, serve with beefsteak.

THE ROYAL BAKING POWDER IS ABSOLUTELY PURE.

Fried Egg Plant.— Peel egg plants, slice thin, sprinkle little salt over them, and let them remain ½ an hour; wipe slices dry, dip them into beaten yelk of egg, then into grated cracker, fry them light brown in boiling lard, seasoning slightly with pepper while they are cooking. Another way is to parboil the egg plants, after they are peeled, in water with a little salt, then slice thin, dust them with corn meal, flour, or corn starch, and fry brown.

How to Serve Melons.—Keep both water and musk melons on ice. Serve by wiping clean the water melon and laying whole upon dish, to be carved at table. If cut up too long before it is to be eaten it becomes insipid. Cut musk melon in two, take out the seeds, and place lump of ice on each half.

Fried Parsnips.— Boil tender in a little hot water, salted; scrape, cut into long slices, dredge with flour, fry in hot lard or dripping. Drain off fat and serve.

Potatoes, Lyonnaise.— Parboil a dozen or more potatoes at breakfast time and set aside after you have peeled them, as they should get perfectly cold. When you are ready to cook them, heat some butter or good dripping in frying-pan; fry in it 1 small onion chopped fine, until it begins to change color—say, one minute or more. Then put in potatoes, cut into small squares (like dice), not too thick or broad. Stir well and cook 5 minutes, taking care potatoes do not break to pieces. *They must not brown.* Put in some minced parsley just before taking up. Drain dry by shaking in a heated colander. Serve very hot.

Potatoes, Stewed.— Pare and cut into lengthwise strips, cover with boiling water, and stew 20 minutes. Turn off nearly all the water, put in a cupful cold milk with salt.

Fried Potatoes.— Time to fry, 10 minutes. Boil potatoes in skins; when cold, peel and cut in slices ¼-inch thick, fry in butter or beef dripping a nice delicate brown. When done, take out, drain grease from them, and serve; or they may be chopped up small, seasoned with pepper and salt, and fried lightly in butter, turning them several times, that they may be nicely browned.

Potato Croquettes.— Season cold mashed potatoes with pepper, salt and nutmeg. Beat to cream, with tablespoonful of melted butter to every cupful of potato. Add 2 or 3 beaten eggs and some minced parsley. Roll into small balls; dip in beaten egg, then in bread crumbs, fry in hot lard.

Baked Potatoes.— Time, 1 hour. Take as many large potatoes as you wish, wash clean, then wipe dry, put them into quick oven for 1 hour. Serve them in napkin, with cold butter, pepper and salt.

Potatoes, Boiled.— Time, from 18 to 20 minutes after water boils; large ones, ½ an hour. Pare potatoes and throw into cold water. Then put into saucepan, cover with cold water, and pinch salt. When the water boils check several times by throwing in cold water, as slower they are boiled the better. When done, throw away water and sprinkle a little salt over them; put at side of fire to dry with lid of saucepan off, then serve quickly with lid of dish raised.

Mashed Potatoes.— Boil potatoes, peel them and break to paste; to 2 pounds of them add ¼ pint milk, a little salt and 2 ounces butter, stir all well over fire. Either serve in this manner, or place them on dish in a form, then brown the top.

Roasted Potatoes.— Select largest, wash and wipe, then bake until soft to grasp — ¾ of an hour usually sufficient time. When done, wipe off ashes and dust, serve in heated napkin.

Saratoga Potatoes.— Take white peachblow potatoes; peel and slice very thin with potato slicer; let stand in cold salt and water for ½ hour; dry them, and fry in boiling hot lard, taking out soon as they rattle against spoon; serve hot.

To Mash Potatoes.— Time, ½ hour, ¾ of an hour if large. Potatoes, a piece of butter, a little milk and salt. Take off skins of potatoes and lay them in cold water for an hour, then put into a saucepan with little salt, cover with water and boil. When done, drain off water, put into bowl and mash fine. Melt piece butter, size of a large egg, with a little milk: mix it well with mashed potatoes until they are a smooth paste, taking care potatoes are not too wet. Then put mash into a dish, piled up; smooth with a knife to serve; or may be improved by browning them in the oven.

Sweet Potato Pie.— Take large sweet potatoes and steam till they are soft, slice thin; pastry is made in usual way, lay potatoes in a deep pie-pan, sprinkle some flour over them, add 2 tablespoonfuls vinegar, 1 teaspoonful butter, ½ teacup water, sugar and nutmeg, or allspice to suit taste. Sweet potato pies should be eaten warm.

Here are Three Ways to Prepare Potatoes for Breakfast.— First, boil some small potatoes in their jackets. The moment they are done take them out of the water. Do not allow them to become soft, as they will not keep their shape. Remove the skins; have some lard, very hot, as for fried cakes; drop the potatoes in and fry till brown, turning them gently from side to side. The next way is to heap mashed potatoes on a small mound or oval platter; shape it like a pyramid and perfectly smooth; then cover with a well-beaten egg, and set it in the oven to brown. Still another way is to make little cakes of cold mashed potatoes; flour your hands well, and put on as much flour as will stick on the outside of the cakes; scatter flour on the plate on which you lay them; fry them brown in butter.

Stewed Mushrooms.— Let them lie in salt and water 1 hour, then cover with fresh water and stew until tender; season with butter, salt and pepper; cream, if you wish.

Fried Tomatoes.— Dip thin slices of ripe tomatoes into flour; salt and pepper them and fry in boiling butter or lard until browned.

Fried Tomatoes.— Cut tomatoes in slices without skinning; pepper and salt them; then sprinkle a little flour over them and fry in butter until brown. Put them on a hot platter and pour milk or cream into the butter and juice. When boiling hot pour over tomatoes.

Stuffed Tomatoes.— Get them as large and firm as possible; cut a round place in top of each, scrape out all the soft parts; mix with stale bread crumbs, corn, onions, parsley, butter, pepper and salt; chop very fine, and fill tomatoes; carefully bake in moderate hot oven; put a little butter in pan; see that they do not burn or become dry.

Stewed Squash.— Pare, seed, quarter, and cook a selected squash soft in boiling salted water. Pour this off; beat squash to pieces in saucepan; season well and stir until stiff and smooth as apple sauce, and it is ready to serve.

Cold Slaw.— 1 quart of finely shaved cabbage, yelks of 3 eggs well beaten, 1½ glassfuls of weak vinegar, 2 teaspoonfuls white sugar, 1 tablespoonful of olive oil, ¼ teacup of thick sweet cream, piece of butter large as a hen's egg, heaping teaspoonful of salt, pepper and mustard. Mix all well together, put over fire till hot, then add cabbage, stew until the whole is heated, place in china dish and set aside to become cold ; add celery or Royal celery salt before serving.

Sauce for Cold Slaw.— 2 eggs well beaten, 1 cup vinegar, 1 teaspoonful of sugar, small piece of butter, and a little mustard if desired. When these are beaten well together, boil and pour over slaw.

Hot Slaw.— Cut a hard white head of cabbage into 2 pieces. Shave 1 piece as fine as possible, and put it into a stewpan with a piece of butter the size of an egg, 1 small teaspoonful salt, and nearly as much pepper. Add ½ teacupful water and 1 teacupful of vinegar. Cover the stewpan and cook the cabbage until it is tender, stirring it often while cooking.

THE ROYAL BAKING POWDER IS ABSOLUTELY PURE.

How to make Sauerkraut. — Barrels having held wine or vinegar are used to prepare the sauerkraut in. It is better, however, to have a special barrel for the purpose. Strasburg, as well as all Alsace, has a well-acquired fame for preparing the cabbages. They slice very white and firm cabbages in fine shreds with a machine made for the purpose. At the bottom of a small barrel they place a layer of coarse salt, and alternately layers of cabbage and salt, being careful to have one of salt on the top. As each layer of cabbage is added, it must be pressed down by a large and heavy pestle, and fresh layers are added as soon as the juice floats on the surface. The cabbage must be seasoned with a few grains of coriander, juniper berries, etc. When the barrel is full it must be put in a dry cellar, covered with a cloth, under a plank, and on this heavy weights are placed. At the end of a few days it will begin to ferment, during which time the pickle must be drawn off and replaced by fresh, until the liquor becomes clear. This should be done every day. Renew the cloth and wash the cover, put the weights back and let stand for a month. By that time the sauerkraut will be ready for use. Care must be taken to let the least air possible enter the sauerkraut, and to have the cover perfectly clean. Each time the barrel has to be opened it must be properly closed again. These precautions must not be neglected.

Celery Minced with Egg Dressing. — Scrape and wash the celery and cut into ½ inch lengths, having first crisped it in cold water. Rub the yelks of 2 eggs (boiled hard) to a paste, with 1 tablespoonful of salad oil ; add salt, pepper, a little powdered sugar, vinegar to make the mixture liquid, and pour over the celery, serve in a salad bowl, and eat at once, lest the celery should toughen in the vinegar.

Celery, Raw. — Wash, trim and scrape the stalks, selecting those that are white and tender, crisp by leaving them in very cold water, until wanted for the table. Arrange neatly in celery stand. Serve between the oysters and meat.

Carrots, Mashed. — Scrape, wash, lay in cold water ½ hour, then cook tender in boiling water. Drain well, mash with a wooden spoon, or beetle, work in a good piece of butter, and season with pepper and salt. Heap up in a vegetable dish ; serve hot.

Carrots, Stewed. — Scrape and boil whole 45 minutes. Drain, and cut in round slices a quarter of an inch thick. Put on in a cupful of weak broth or soup, and cook gently ½ hour. Then add 3 or 4 tablespoonfuls of milk, a lump of butter rolled in flour, with seasoning to taste. Boil up and dish.

Succotash. — 8 ears corn, cut off grains, 1 pint Lima beans, 1 tablespoonful floured butter. pepper and salt, 1 cup milk. Boil corn and beans nearly an hour in enough water to cover them ; turn this off, and the milk ; when this heats, butter, pepper and salt. Simmer 10 minutes.

Succotash No. 2. — Cut the corn from 10 cobs ; mix this with one-third the quantity of Lima beans, and cook 1 hour in just enough water to cover them. Drain off most of the water ; add a cupful of milk, with a pinch of soda stirred in. When this boils, stir in a great spoonful of butter rolled in flour ; season with pepper and salt, and simmer 10 minutes longer.

Green Corn Boiled Whole. — Strip off the outer husks ; turn down the innermost covering ; pull off the silk with great care. Re-cover the ear with the thin inner husk ; tie at the top with a bit of thread, and cook in salted boiling water ½ hour. Cut off the stalks close to the cob, and serve wrapped in a napkin.

Stewed Tomatoes With Onion and Bread. — Empty can tomatoes into a saucepan, place over fire, and when hot add small onion sliced, with pepper, salt and a little sugar. Stew 20 minutes, and add tablespoonful butter and a good handful bread crumbs. Simmer 5 or 10 minutes, and pour out.

Stewed Corn. — Stew 1 quart canned corn in its own liquor, setting the vessel containing it in another of hot water. Should the corn be too dry, add a little cold water. When tender, pour in enough milk to cover the corn ; bring to a boil ; put in 1 tablespoonful butter rolled in flour, and salt to taste. Stew gently, stirring well, 3 or 4 minutes, and turn into a deep dish. Keep the vessel containing the corn closely covered while it is cooking. The steam facilitates the process and preserves the color of the corn.

Green Corn Cut From the Cob. — After boiling, cut the corn, with a sharp knife, from the cob, into a hot dish ; stir in butter, pepper and salt, and cover to keep hot until eaten.

Stewed Tomatoes, Plain. — Open a can of tomatoes an hour before cooking them ; scald out cores ; cook always in a tin or porcelain saucepan. Iron injures both color and flavor. Stew gently for forty minutes ; season to taste with salt, pepper, and, if preferred, a little sugar, and 1 tablespoonful butter. Cook gently, uncovered, 10 minutes longer, and turn into a deep dish.

Raw Tomatoes. — Peel and slice with a sharp knife. (Tomatoes should always be cut just before using.) Lay in salad bowl and season with dressing, made in following proportions : Beat together 4 tablespoonfuls vinegar, 1 teaspoonful each of salt and sugar, half as much mustard, and when these are well mixed, add gradually 2 tablespoonfuls best salad oil.

Corned Beef and Turnips. — Cook the beef in plenty cold water, bringing slowly to a boil. Cook 15 minutes to the pound after it begins to simmer. When about ¾ done put in a dozen turnips, peeled and quartered. When you dish the beef lay these unmashed about. Serve meat with drawn butter, having as a base the pot liquor. Remainder of liquor can be saved for next day's soup.

Boiled Cauliflower. — Cook in boiling salted water 25 minutes, having tied the cauliflower up in white netting. Drain, untie ; lay in a deep dish, the blossom upward, and deluge white sauce made of drawn butter, with the juice of a lemon squeezed in.

Spinach with Egg. — Boil spinach in plenty hot water, salted, for 20 minutes. Drain and press out the water. Chop fine ; put back over the fire with a large spoonful butter, and a teaspoonful sugar, with salt and pepper to taste, also a little nutmeg. Beat until hot and smooth ; turn into a hot, deep dish, and cover with a dressing of the yelks of 4 hard boiled eggs ; left to cool, then pounded in a Wedgewood mortar, and rubbed to a paste, with a teaspoonful melted butter, one of cream, and, lastly, one of lemon juice. Spread over surface of the spinach, and garnish with a border of the sliced whites of the eggs.

Green Peas. — Shell the peas and wash well in cold water. Cook in boiling water for 25 minutes. A lump of sugar will be a pleasant addition to market peas. Drain well ; stir in a great lump of butter, and pepper and salt. Serve hot.

Canned Peas. — Open can peas 1 hour before cooking them, and turn into a bowl. When ready for them, put on in a farina-kettle — or one saucepan within another — of hot water. If dry, add cold water to cover them, and stew about 25 minutes. Drain ; stir in a generous lump of butter, pepper and salt.

Onions, Baked. — Cook in two waters, the second salted and boiling ; when tender drain ; set closely together in a bake dish ; pepper, butter and salt liberally ; pour over them a little soupstock strained through a cloth ; brown in a good oven ; lay in a deep dish, and pour over them the gravy thickened with browned flour, and cook one minute.

Rice, Boiled. — Wash well and cook in hot salted water, shaking up from time to time until the water is nearly all absorbed, and the rice soft, with every grain distinct ; put a good piece of butter on the top after it is dished.

THE ROYAL BAKING POWDER IS ABSOLUTELY PURE.

Boiled Onions. — Clear off top and tail ; skin and cook 15 minutes in boiling fresh water ; salt slightly and boil until tender all through ; drain, butter well, and pepper and salt.

String Beans. — If fresh, top and tail, and with a sharp knife take off the strings on both sides ; cut into short pieces, and cook tender in boiling water, and a little salt ; drain well ; heap upon a hot dish ; butter freely, and season to taste.

Boiled Beans. — Soak all night, and in the morning change the cold water for luke-warm ; let stand in this 2 hours ; drain off, and put them to boil in cold water, with a piece of fat salt pork 2 inches square. Cook slowly until soft : take out the pork ; drain the beans well ; season with pepper, and serve.

Onions, Boiled, with Sauce. — Boil 15 minutes in salted water. Throw this off ; add a little gravy : if none ready, make as follows : Boil a chicken scrag and feet in a pint water, until there is less than a cupful of broth ; season and thicken this with chopped parsley. Stew 5 minutes longer, or until tender, and serve.

Onions, Fried. — After clearing off tops and tails, slice them with a sharp knife ; place in pan with beef dripping or good butter. Stir and shake them until they begin to brown. If served with steak, dish and lay the onions on top of the steak ; cover, and let stand where they will keep hot, for 5 minutes, then serve.

Beets. — Use care in cutting off the tops and washing them not to break the skins, or they will bleed away their color in the water. Cook in boiling water 1 hour. Scrape, slice, salt, pepper and butter, and pour a few spoonfuls of boiling vinegar upon them after they are dished.

Eggs and Asparagus. — Cut about 2 dozen stalks of asparagus, leaving out the hard parts, into inch lengths, and boil tender. Drain ; pour upon them a cupful drawn butter ; stir until hot, then turn into a bake dish. Break 6 eggs upon the top : put a bit of butter upon each ; salt and pepper, and put into a quick oven until the eggs are " set."

Eggs with Mushrooms. — Slice the mushrooms from cans into halves. Stew 10 minutes in a little butter seasoned with pepper and salt, and a very little water. Drain, put the mushrooms into a pie dish ; break enough eggs to cover them over the top ; pepper, salt, and scatter bits of butter over them ; strew with bread crumbs, and bake until the eggs are " set." Serve in the dish.

Squash, Stewed. — Pare, slice, lay in cold water 15 minutes. Cook tender in boiling water, salted : drain well, and mash with pepper, salt and butter, pressing out all the water.

Squash, Mashed. — Peel, seed, and slice fresh summer squashes. Lay in cold water 10 minutes ; put in boiling water, a little salt, and cook tender — 20 minutes, if the squash be young. Mash in a colander, pressing out all the water ; heap in a deep dish, seasoning with pepper, salt, and butter. Serve hot.

Ragoût of Vegetables. — Parboil 1 carrot, 1 turnip, 2 potatoes, 2 ears of corn, 1 cup of Lima beans, and the same of peas, 1 onion, and with them ¼ pound of fat salt pork. Drain off the water and lay aside the pork. Slice carrots, turnips, potatoes, and onion. Put into a saucepan with a cup of some good meat soup before it has been thickened. Season well ; cut the corn from the cob and add with the peas, beans, and a sliced tomato as soon as the rest are hot. Stew all together ½ hour. Stir in a great lump of butter rolled in flour. Stew 5 minutes, and serve in a deep dish.

Raw Cucumbers. — Pare and lay them in ice water 1 hour, then slice and season to taste with vinegar, pepper, and salt. Never omit the soaking in ice water.

Bananas and Oranges. — Serve in same fruit basket or dish.

Baked Hominy. — 1 cupful of cold hominy (small grained), 2 cups milk, 1 large teaspoonful each butter and sugar, little salt, 2 eggs. Work the melted butter well into the hominy, mashing all lumps, then the beaten yelks ; next sugar and salt ; then gradually the milk ; lastly the whites. Beat until perfectly smooth, and bake in a greased pudding dish until delicately browned. Serve in the bake dish.

Rice Croquettes. — 1 cup of cold boiled rice. 1 teaspoonful of sugar and half as much salt, 1 teaspoonful melted butter, 1 egg beaten light, enough milk to make the rice into stiff paste. Sweet lard for frying. Work rice, butter, egg, etc., into an adhesive paste, beating each ingredient thoroughly into the mixture. Flour your hands and make the rice into oval balls. Dip each in beaten egg, then in flour or cracker dust, and fry in boiling lard, a few at a time, turning each with great care. When the croquettes are of a fine yellow brown, take out with a wire spoon and lay within a heated colander to drain off every drop of fat. Serve hot, with sprigs of parsley laid about them, in an uncovered dish.

Rice, Baked. — Wash a cup of rice well. Take cup broth, strain through a thin cloth, and add twice as much boiling water, with a little salt. Put in the rice, and cook slowly until it has taken up all the water and is soft. Pour in a large cup of hot milk, in which have been mixed 2 eggs (raw), 2 tablespoonfuls grated cheese and a tablespoonful butter. Stir up well ; add about cupful minced veal and ham, taken from your soup, turn into a greased mould ; cover and bake 1 hour in a dripping-pan of hot water, dip in cold water and invert upon a flat dish.

Stewed Potatoes. — Pare and cut potatoes into quarters, and these into long, even strips. Lay in cold water ½ hour, and cook in boiling water until tender, with half a minced onion. Drain off nearly all the water ; pepper and salt, and add a cup cold milk, with a tablespoonful butter rolled in flour. When it thickens, stir in a little chopped parsley. Simmer 5 minutes and serve. Potatoes should not be allowed to break so much as to lose their shape.

Stewed Salsify. — Scrape and cut each root in two, scrape them and drop into water. Stew in boiling water, a little salt, until tender ; pour off the water, add enough milk to cover the roots ; when it boils, stir in a piece of butter rolled in flour. pepper and salt : simmer 5 minutes, and pour out.

Fried Salsify. — Scrape and lay in cold water 10 minutes. Boil tender, drain, and when cold mash with a wooden spoon, picking out the fibrous parts. Wet to a paste with milk, work in a little butter, and 1½ eggs for each cupful of salsify. Beat the eggs very light, season to taste, make into round flat cakes, dredge with flour, and fry to a light brown, drain off the fat and serve hot.

Pickles.

CHOW CHOW. 1 quart large cucumbers, 1 quart small cucumbers, 2 quarts onions, 4 heads cauliflower, 6 green peppers, 1 quart green tomatoes, 1 gallon vinegar, 1 pound mustard, 2 cups sugar, 2 cups flour, 1 ounce turmeric. Put all in salt and water one night ; cook all the vegetables in brine until tender, except large cucumbers. Pour over vinegar and spices.

Pickling Cauliflowers. — Take whitest and closest cauliflowers in bunches ; spread on earthen dish, cover them with salt, and let stand 3 days to draw out all the water. Then put in jars, pour boiling salt and water over them, let stand over night ; then drain with a hair sieve, and put in glass jars ; fill up jars with vinegar ; cover tight.

East India Pickles.—100 cucumbers (large and small), 1 peck green tomatoes, ½ peck onions, 4 cauliflowers, 4 red peppers (without seeds), 4 heads celery, 1 pint bottle horse-radish. Slice all, stand in salt twenty-four hours; then drain, pour over weak vinegar, stand on stove until it comes to a boil, then drain again. 1 ounce ground cinnamon, 1 ounce ground turmeric, pound mustard, ¼ pound brown sugar; wet these with cold vinegar; add sufficient vinegar to moisten all the pickles. Cook all together 10 minutes. Seal in bottles while hot.

French Pickles.—1 peck green tomatoes, sliced; 6 large onions, a teacup salt thrown on over night. Drain thoroughly, boil in 2 quarts water and 1 quart vinegar 15 or 20 minutes; drain in colander; then take 4 quarts vinegar, 2 pounds brown sugar, ½ pound white mustard seed, 2 tablespoonfuls cloves, 2 tablespoonfuls cinnamon, 2 tablespoonfuls ginger, 2 tablespoonfuls ground mustard, 1 teaspoonful cayenne pepper; put all together, cook 15 minutes.

Mangoes.—Take small musk melons and cut an oval piece out of one side; take out the seeds with teaspoon, and fill this space with stuffing of chopped onion, scraped horse-radish, mustard seed, cloves, and whole pepper; sew in the piece. Put in jar, pour boiling vinegar, with a little salt in it, over them. Do this 3 times, then put in fresh vinegar, cover close.

Pickles.—Use glass bottles for pickles, also wooden knives and forks in preparation of them. Fill bottles 3 parts full with articles to be pickled, then fill bottle with vinegar. Use saucepans lined with earthenware, or stone pipkins, to boil vinegar in.

Piccalilly.—1 peck green tomatoes, sliced; ½ peck onions, sliced; 1 cauliflower, 1 peck small cucumbers. Leave in salt and water 24 hours; then put in kettle with handful scraped horse-radish, 1 ounce turmeric, 1 ounce cloves (whole), ¼ pound pepper (whole), 1 ounce cassia buds or cinnamon, 1 pound white mustard seed, 1 pound English mustard. Place in kettle in layers, and cover with cold vinegar. Boil 15 minutes, constantly stirring.

Pickled Mussels.—Boil them as directed in the previous receipt, put them in glass jars, and cover them with vinegar heated scalding hot, with whole pepper, mace, and allspice.

Pickled Peaches.—Take ripe, but not too soft peaches, put a clove into one end of each peach. Take 2 pounds brown sugar to gallon of vinegar, skim and boil up twice; pour it hot over peaches and cover close. In a week or two pour off and scald vinegar again. After this they will keep any length of time.

Pickled Red Cabbage.—Slice it into a colander, sprinkle each layer with salt; let it drain 2 days, then put into a jar, pour boiling vinegar enough to cover, put in few slices of red beet-root. Choose purple red cabbage. Those who like flavor of spice will boil it, with the vinegar. Cauliflower cut in bunches, and thrown in after being salted, will look red and beautiful.

To Pickle Cucumbers.—Take 200 or 300, lay them on a dish, salt, and let them remain 8 or 9 hours; then drain, laying them in a jar, pour boiling vinegar upon them. Place near the fire, covered with vine-leaves. If they do not become sufficiently green, strain off the vinegar, boil it, and again pour it over them, covering with fresh leaves. Continue till they become green as you wish.

To Pickle Tomatoes.—Always use those that are thoroughly ripe. The small round ones are decidedly the best. Do not prick them, as most books direct. Let them lie in strong brine three or four days, then put down in layers in jars, mixing with small onions and pieces of horse-radish. Then pour on vinegar (cold), which should be first spiced; let there be a spice-bag to throw into every pot. Cover carefully, and set by in cellar full month before using.

Sweet Pickle for Plums, Peaches or Tomatoes.—4 quarts cider vinegar, 5 pounds sugar, ¼ pound cinnamon, 2 ounces cloves to 7 pounds fruit. Scald the vinegar and sugar together and skim, add spices, boil up once, and pour over the fruit. Pour off and scald vinegar twice more at intervals of three days, and then cover all close. A less expensive way: Take 4 pounds sugar to 8 pounds of fruit, 2 ounces cinnamon, 1 ounce cloves, 1 teaspoonful salt, 1 teaspoonful allspice.

Catsups.

GREEN TOMATO CATSUP.—1 peck green tomatoes, 1 dozen large onions, ½ pint salt; slice tomatoes and onions. To layer of these add layer of salt; let stand 24 hours, then drain. Add ¼ pound mustard seed, 3 dessert-spoons sweet oil, 1 ounce allspice, 1 ounce cloves, 1 ounce ground mustard, 1 ounce ground ginger, 2 tablespoonfuls black pepper, 2 teaspoonfuls celery seed, ¼ pound brown sugar. Put all in preserving pan, cover with vinegar, and boil 2 hours.

Tomato Catsup.—1 peck ripe tomatoes, cut up, boil tender and sift through wire sieve; add 1 large tablespoonful ground cloves, 1 large tablespoonful allspice, 1 large tablespoonful cinnamon, 1 teaspoonful cayenne pepper, ¼ pound salt, ¼ pound mustard, 1 pint vinegar. Boil gently 3 hours. Bottle and seal while warm.

Tomato Catsup.—1 gallon tomatoes (strained), 6 tablespoonfuls salt, 3 tablespoonfuls black pepper, 1 tablespoonful cloves, 2 tablespoonfuls cinnamon, 2 tablespoonfuls allspice, 1½ pints vinegar; boil down one-half. 1 peck tomatoes will make 1 gallon strained.

Tomato Soy.—½ peck tomatoes, 1 large pepper cut fine, 1 large onion cut in slices, 1 tablespoonful each of ground allspice, black pepper and celery seed, ¼ cup of salt, ½ pint of vinegar. Boil all together slowly 1 hour; cool, and bottle for use.

Walnut Catsup.—Take green walnuts before the shell is formed (usually in a proper state early in August). Grind them or pound them in an earthen or marble mortar. Squeeze out the juice through a coarse cloth, and add to every gallon of juice 1 pound of anchovies, 1 pound salt, 4 ounces cayenne pepper, 2 ounces black pepper, 1 ounce each ginger, cloves and mace, and the root of one horse-radish. Boil all together till reduced to half the quantity. Pour off, and when cold bottle tight. Use in 3 months.

Spiced Fruits.

BRANDY PEACHES.—Drop peaches in hot water, let them remain till skin can be ripped off; make thin syrup, let it cover fruit; boil fruit till they can be pierced with a straw; take it out, make very rich syrup, and add, after it is taken from fire, while it is still hot, an equal quantity of brandy. Pour while still warm over the peaches in the jar. Peaches must be covered with it.

Canned Pineapple.—Pare fruit—be very particular to cut out eyes. Weigh and chop fine. Add same weight of sugar. Mix thoroughly in large crock, let it stand 24 hours. Then put in cans, fill full, seal tight. After leaving them about 3 weeks look and see if any signs of working. If so, pour into pan, warm through, then replace in cans.

Spiced Tomatoes.—20 pounds of ripe tomatoes scalded and peeled, 2 quarts of vinegar, 8 pounds of sugar, 4 tablespoonfuls each of cinnamon, cloves, and allspice. Boil till thick, stirring often.

Spiced Currants.—5 pounds currants, 4 lbs. brown sugar, 2 tablespoonfuls cloves, 2 tablespoonfuls cinnamon, 1 pint vinegar; boil 2 hours or till quite thick.

Spiced Peaches.—7 pounds fruit, 1 pint vinegar, 3 pounds sugar, 2 ounces cinnamon, ½ ounce cloves. Scald together sugar, vinegar and spices; pour over the fruit. Let stand 24 hours; drain off, scald again and pour over fruit, letting it stand another 24 hours. Boil all together until fruit is tender. Skim it and boil liquor until thickened. Pour over fruit and set away in jar.

Spiced Grapes.—7 pounds grapes, 3 pounds sugar, 1 pint vinegar, 1 tablespoonful cloves, 1 tablespoonful cinnamon.

Spiced Elderberries.—Take 9 lbs. cleaned elderberries, 3 lbs. brown sugar, 1 pint vinegar, 1 ounce cloves, 1 ounce allspice, 1 ounce cinnamon; put sugar and vinegar in a 2-gallon brass or copper kettle, and place it on the stove; let it come to a boil; then add berries and let it boil 2½ hours; when done grind spice, and tie in little bags and put in; simmer a few minutes; take off and seal in cans.

Pickled Peaches or Pears.—1 quart vinegar to 4½ lbs. sugar, ½ lb. sugar to little over 1 lb. fruit; place all the sugar and vinegar over the fire till it comes to a boil; then lay a layer of fruit and cook until soft enough to run a fork through; then remove the fruit and fill the same way until all are done; the syrup needs no more cooking; before cooking the fruit, stick 4 cloves in each.

Cordials.

BLACKBERRY CORDIAL.—Simmer blackberries till they break; strain, and to each pint of juice put a pound of white sugar, ¼ ounce cinnamon, ¼ ounce mace, 2 teaspoonfuls Royal Extract *Cloves*. Boil 15 minutes, and when cool add a little brandy, though brandy is not an essential. Other fruit cordials in the same way.

Blackberry Wine.—Berries should be ripe and plump. Put into a large wood or stone vessel with a tap. Pour on sufficient boiling water to cover them. When cool enough to bear your hand bruise well until all the berries are broken. Cover up, let stand till berries begin to rise to top, which will occur in 3 or 4 days. Then draw off the clear juice in another vessel, and add 1 pound sugar to every 10 quarts of the liquor, and stir thoroughly. Let stand 6 to 10 days in first vessel with tap. Then draw off through a jelly bag. Steep 4 ounces isinglass in a pint white wine for 12 hours; boil it over sl ow fire till all dissolve, then place dissolved isinglass in a gallon of blackberry juice, give them a boil together, and pour all into the vessel. Let stand few days to ferment and settle, draw off and keep in cool place. Make all other berry wines in s me manner.

Roman Punch.—Make 2 quarts lemonade, rich with pure juice lemon fruit; add 1 tablespoonful Royal Extract *Lemon*. Work well and freeze; just before serving, add for each quart of ice, ½ pint brandy, and 1½ pint Jamaica rum. Mix well and serve in high glasses, as this makes what is called a semi or half ice. It is usually served at dinners as a *coup de milieu*.

Noyeau Cordial.—To 1 gallon of proof spirit add 3 pounds of loaf sugar and a tablespoonful of Royal Extract *Almonds*. Mix well together and allow to stand 48 hours, covered closely; now strain through thick flannel, and bottle. This liquor will be much improved by adding ½ pint of apricot or peach juice.

Orange Sherbet.—5 quarts of water, 4 pounds granulated sugar, 4 beaten eggs, juice and grated rinds of 4 oranges and juice of 2 lemons. Beat sugar and eggs together, then add water and grated rinds. Freeze like ice cream. The strained juice of oranges and lemons should not be added until the mixture begins to freeze.

Some Choice Menus

AS SPECIMENS.

PUBLISHED IN THE NEW-YORK "HERALD" CHRISTMAS DAY.

SERVICE CHAUD.
Consommé en tasses.
Croquette de volaille.
Terrapin à la Maryland.

SERVICE FROID, GROSSES PIECES.
Bass rayée à la Magellen.
Filet de bœuf à la Noël.
Volière de faisans à la Buffon.
Pâtés de gibier à la Bacchus.
Salade de homard.   Salade de volaille.
Grosses pièces de pâtisseries.
Gâteau Sicilien historié.
Ice Cream.   Nougat.   St. Nicolas.
Gâteaux.   Dessert.

Epicurean bachelors, with no tables of their own, will feast as follows at a club famed for its *cuisine*.

Oysters.
Green turtle clear.   Purée à la Reine.
Petites Timballes à la Talleyrand.
Striped bass à la Chambord.
Cucumbers.
Roast saddle Southdown mutton.
Pommes Duchesse.   Choux de Bruxelle.
Suprême de volaille à l'Ambassadrice.
Petits pois.
Chesapeake Terrapin à la Maryland.
Sorbet au Kirsch.
Roast canvas-back ducks.
Hominy balls.   Lettuce salad.
Fromages variés.
Neapolitan ice cream.
Fruit.   Café.   Liqueurs.

A leading hotel offers its guests to-day this liberal repast for dinner:—

OYSTERS ON HALF SHELL.
SOUPS.
A la Reine.   Vermicelli.
FISH.
Salmon trout, à la Bechamel.
Broiled fresh mackerel, parsley sauce.
Small potatoes.
BOILED.
Leg of mutton, caper sauce.
Corned beef and cabbage.
Chicken and pork.   Calf's head, brain sauce.
Beef tongue.   Ham.
COLD DISHES.
Beef tongue.   A la mode beef.   Roast beef.
Boned turkey.   Chicken salad.   Lobster salad.
Plain lobster.   Ham.
ENTREES.
Terrapin à la Maryland.
Fricaseed chicken, à la chevalier.
Oysters baked in the shell.
Broiled quail on toast.
Noix of beef, with vegetables.
Macaroni, with Parmesan cheese.
ROAST.
Chicken. Ham, champagne sauce. Mongrel goose.
Beef.   Saddle of mutton.   Turkey.
GAME.
Redhead duck.
VEGETABLES.
Boiled potatoes, stewed tomatoes, onions, mashed potatoes, sweet potatoes, squash, beets, fried oyster plant, Lima beans, rice, spinach, corn.
PASTRY.
English plum pudding, wine sauce.
Rice pudding.   Mince pie.
Vienna tarts.   Pumpkin pie.
Christmas cakes.   Charlotte Russe. Almond cake.
Lady's cake.
DESSERT.
Bananas, pears, grapes, apples, raisins, Hickory nuts, oranges, almonds, English walnuts, Pecan nuts, vanilla ice cream, Roman punch.
Coffee.

THE ROYAL BAKING POWDER IS ABSOLUTELY PURE.

Ice Cream and Fruit Ices.

In all Ice Cream Receipts, Eggs can be Left Out if Desirable.

BISCUIT GLACE. — 1½ pints cream, 12 ounces sugar, 8 yelks of eggs, and 1 tablespoonful Royal Extract of *Vanilla*. Take 6 ounces crisp macaroons, pound in mortar to dust. Mix cream, sugar, eggs, and extract. Place on fire, and stir composition until it begins to thicken. Strain and rub through hair sieve into basin. Put into freezer; when nearly frozen, mix in macaroon dust. Another tablespoonful Royal Extract *Vanilla*, and finish freezing.

Coffee Ice Cream. — 1 quart best cream, ½ pint of strong Mocha coffee, 14 ounces white pulverized sugar, yelks 8 eggs. Mix these ingredients in a porcelain-lined basin. Place on fire to thicken. Rub through hair sieve into a basin. Put into freezer and freeze.

Chocolate Ice Cream, No. 1. - 3 pints best cream, 12 ounces pulverized white sugar, 4 whole eggs, a tablespoonful Royal Extract *Vanilla*, a pint rich cream whipped, 6 ounces chocolate. Dissolve chocolate in small quantity of milk to smooth paste. Now mix it with cream, sugar, eggs, and Royal extract. Place all on fire, stir until it begins to thicken. Strain through hair sieve. Place in freezer; when nearly frozen, stir in lightly the whipped cream, and 1 tablespoonful Royal Extract *Vanilla*, and finish.

Chocolate Ice Cream, No. 2. — 1 quart rich sweet cream, ½ pound granulated sugar, 2 ounces chocolate flavored with 2 teaspoonfuls of Royal Extract *Vanilla*. Be very careful to have chocolate rubbed to smooth paste by having milk warm and adding very small quantity at a time. Add all together and freeze.

Crushed Strawberry Ice Cream. — 3 pints best cream, 12 ounces pulverized white sugar, 2 whole eggs. Mix all in porcelain-lined basin; place on fire; stir constantly to boiling point. Remove and strain through hair sieve. Place in freezer and freeze. Take 1 quart ripe strawberries, select, hull, and put in a china bowl. Add 6 ounces pulverized white sugar, crush all down to pulp. Add this pulp to frozen cream, with 2 tablespoonfuls Royal Extract *Vanilla*, mix in well. Now give freezer few additional turns to harden.

French Vanilla Ice Cream. — 1 quart rich sweet cream, ½ pound granulated sugar, yelks of 6 eggs. Place cream and sugar in porcelain kettle on fire, allow them to come to boil; strain immediately through hair sieve, and having the eggs well beaten, add them slowly to the cream and sugar while hot, at some time stirring rapidly. Place on fire again and stir for few minutes. Then pour into the freezer and flavor with 1 tablespoonful Royal Extract *Vanilla*, and freeze.

Italian Orange Ice Cream. — 1½ pints best cream, 12 ounces white pulverized sugar, juice of 6 oranges, 2 teaspoonfuls Royal Extract *Orange*, yelks of 8 eggs, and pinch of salt. Mix these ingredients in porcelain-lined basin, stir over fire until the composition begins to thicken. Rub and pass the cream through a hair sieve, put into freezer and freeze.

Lemon Ice Cream. — 1 quart best cream, 8 ounces white pulverized sugar, 3 whole eggs. Place on fire. Stir continually, until it reaches boiling point. Then immediately remove and strain. When cold, place in freezer, and flavor with 1 tablespoonful Royal Extract *Lemon*, and freeze.

Lemon Water Ice. — Juice 6 lemons, 2 teaspoonfuls Royal Extract *Lemon*, 1 quart water, 1 pound powdered sugar, 1 gill rich, sweet cream; add altogether and strain. Freeze same as *Ice Cream*.

Orange Water Ice. — Juice 6 oranges, 2 teaspoonfuls Royal Extract *Orange*, juice of 1 lemon, 1 quart water, 1 pound powdered sugar, 1 gill rich, sweet cream; add altogether and strain. Freeze same as *Ice Cream*.

Peach Ice Cream. — One dozen of best and ripest red-cheeked peaches: peel and stone: place in china basin, crush with 6 ounces pulverized sugar. Now take 1 quart best cream, 8 ounces pulverized white sugar, 2 whole eggs. Place all on fire until it reaches boiling point; now remove and strain; place in freezer and freeze. When nearly frozen stir in peach pulp, with teaspoonful Royal Extract *Almond*; give few more turns of freezer to harden.

Raspberry Water Ice. — Press sufficient raspberries through hair sieve to give 3 pints of juice. Add 1 pound pulverized white sugar, and juice of 1 lemon, with one teaspoonful Royal Extract *Raspberry*. Place in freezer and freeze.

Red Currant Fruit Ice. — Put 3 pints of ripe currants, 1 pint red raspberries, ½ pint of water in basin. Place on fire and allow to simmer for few minutes, then strain through hair sieve. To this add 12 ounces sugar, and ½ pint of water. Place all into freezing can and freeze.

Beverages.

CHOCOLATE. — 1 tablespoonful chocolate for each person. Pour on boiling water and allow to thicken up; milk enough to cool; then stir in well beaten egg and sugar to taste; add milk and boil 10 to 20 minutes; flavor with Royal Extract *Vanilla*. Beat whites of eggs and pour over when ready to serve.

Cocoa. — 6 tablespoonfuls cocoa to each pint water, as much milk as water, sugar to taste. Rub cocoa smooth in little cold water: have ready on the fire pint boiling water; stir in grated cocoa paste. Boil 20 minutes, add milk and boil 5 minutes more, stirring often. Sweeten in cups so as to suit different tastes.

Coffee for Six Persons. — Take 1 full cup ground coffee, 1 egg, a little cold water; stir together, add 1 pint boiling water, boil up; then add another pint boiling water, and set back to settle before serving.

French Coffee, No. 1. — 3 pints water to 1 cupful ground coffee. Put coffee grounds in bowl; pour over it about ½ pint cold water and let stand for 15 minutes; bring remaining 2½ pints water to a boil. Take coffee in bowl, strain through fine sieve, then take French coffee-pot, put coffee grounds in strainer at top of French pot, leaving water in bowl. Then take boiling water and pour over coffee very slowly. Then set coffee-pot on stove 5 minutes; *must not boil*. Take off and pour in cold water from bowl that coffee was first soaked in to settle. Serve in another pot. The French, who have the reputation of making the best coffee, use 3 parts Java, 1 part Mocha.

Koumiss. — (*Sometimes called Milk Beer*).—Into 1 quart of new milk put 1 gill of fresh buttermilk and 3 or 4 lumps of white sugar. Mix well and see that the sugar dissolves. Put in warm place to stand 10 hours, when it will be thick. Pour from one vessel to another until it becomes smooth and uniform in consistency. Bottle and keep in warm place 24 hours; it may take 36 in winter. The bottles must be tightly corked and the corks tied down. Shake well 5 minutes before opening. It makes a very agreeable drink, which is especially recommended for persons who do not assimilate their food, and for young children may be drank as freely as milk. Instead of buttermilk, some use a teaspoonful of yeast. It is the standard beverage of the Tartars, who almost live upon it in summer, and is also used largely by the Russians. The richer your milk, which should be unskimmed, the better will be your koumiss.

THE ROYAL BAKING POWDER IS ABSOLUTELY PURE.

French Coffee, No. 2. — 1½ cups ground coffee. Put in a flannel bag, tie top and put in old fashioned coffee-pot ; pour on 3 pints water, boil 10 minutes ; serve in another coffee-pot. A very rich coffee can be made by adding to grounds first placed in bowl 1 egg, shell and all broken, and thoroughly mixed with coffee. Where egg is used omit soaking coffee grounds in water.

Vienna Coffee. — Equal parts Mocha and Java coffee ; allow 1 heaping tablespoonful of coffee to each person, and 2 extra to make good strength. Mix 1 egg with grounds, pour on coffee ½ as much boiling water as will be needed, let coffee froth, then stir down grounds and let boil 5 minutes ; then let coffee stand where it will keep hot, but not boil, for 5 or 10 minutes, and add rest of water. To one pint of cream add white of an egg, well beaten ; this is to be put in cups with sugar, and hot coffee added.

Maple Beer. — To 4 gallons boiling water put 1 quart maple syrup, and 1 tablespoonful essence of spruce ; when about milk-warm add 1 pint yeast ; when fermented, bottle it. In 3 days it will be fit for use.

Tea. — To make good tea is almost as difficult as to make good coffee ; the failure in both cases usually comes from not using good and sufficient material. Following receipt makes good tea : Scald teapot, put in plenty tea, cover with boiling water, spread thick napkin over and about it and let stand 5 minutes before filling with more boiling water ; let stand 10 or 12 minutes longer, and pour out.

Iced Tea. — Mixed tea makes a better cold drink than either black or green. Strain it into perfectly clean bottle and keep on ice. When a drink is wanted, pour glass ¾ full, sweeten lavishly and fill up glass with broken ice. Drink without cream.

Cookery for the Sick.

FOOD FOR THE SICK. — Always prepare food for the sick in the neatest and most careful manner. In sickness the senses are unusually acute, and far more susceptible to carelessness, negligences and mistakes in the preparation and serving of food than when in health. Special wants of the body show themselves in special cravings for certain articles of food. These should be gratified when possible.

Formula for making Beef Tea approved by the Board of Physicians of the Brooklyn, N. Y., Diet Dispensary.

Beef Tea. — To every pound of beef, cut fine (not chopped), add 1 pint cold water, and let stand 2 hours ; then place over a slow fire, or place on the extreme back part of a range, where it may heat through very gradually ; then pull forward where it may come quickly to a simmer, or just below the boiling point. Stir thoroughly at intervals of about 10 minutes. In 2 hours from time it is placed over the fire it may be considered done, although no harm will be done if it remain ½ hour longer, provided it does not boil ; strain through a colander into an earthen bowl. Strain the second time through a fine tin strainer. If it has been properly cooked and not allowed to boil or get hot too quickly, there will remain but little sediment from the last straining. If, on the other hand, these rules have not been observed, the body and substance of the meat will remain in the strainer, leaving a thin watery mixture of little value. Practice and watchful care only will enable the cook to bring the beef tea up to the boiling point without letting it boil. This is the test of the article. Do not salt while cooking, as that causes it to separate.

Bouillon Soup. — See under heading *Soups and Broths.*

Calf's Feet Jelly. — Boil 2 calf's feet, well cleaned, in 1 gallon water until reduced to 1 quart, then pour out into a pan. When cold skim off all the fat and take up the jelly, leaving what settling may remain at the bottom. Put the jelly into a saucepan. Pour over it 1 pint good Sherry or Madeira wine, ½ pound white sugar, and the juice of four lemons. Add to these whites of 6 or 8 eggs well beaten together. Stir all together thoroughly, place on fire and let boil a few minutes. Pour into a large flannel bag, and repeat this until it runs clear ; then have ready a large china basin, and drop in it some lemon peel cut as thin as possible. Let the jelly run into the basin ; the lemon peel will not only give it a pleasing color but a grateful flavor. Fill your glasses, and it will be ready to use.

Chicken Broth. — See under heading of *Soups and Broths.*

Egg on Toast. — Brown a slice of bread nicely over the coals, and while doing this break an egg into boiling water, and let it stand over the fire till the white hardens. Butter the toast, take up the egg with a skimmer, lay it on the toast and serve.

Flaxseed Tea. — Upon an ounce of unbruised flaxseed and a little pulverized liquorice root pour a pint of boiling (soft or rain) water, and place the vessel containing these ingredients near, but not on, the fire for 4 hours. Strain through a linen cloth. Make it fresh every day. An excellent drink in fever accompanied by a cough.

Infants' Food. — Let 1 quart of milk stand over night ; skim off the cream, and upon it pour 1 pint of boiling water. In 1 quart of water let 1 tablespoonful of oatmeal boil about 2 hours and then strain. To 1 gill of the cream and water add 2 tablespoonfuls of the oatmeal water. Sweeten it when given. This receipt comes from an experienced nurse, and has been well tested.

Mint Tea. — In an earthen vessel put a handful of the young shoots of mint, pour over them boiling water, cover closely and let it set near the fire for an hour. Other herb teas are made in the same way. Mint tea is useful in allaying nausea and vomiting.

Mutton Broth. — 3 pounds of lean mutton, 2 turnips, 1 carrot, 2 onions, 1 bunch parsley, 1 cup milk, 1 tablespoonful corn starch, 3 quarts water. Boil meat, cut into strips, and the vegetables, sliced, in the water 2½ hours. The water should be reduced ⅓. Strain, taking out the meat, and rubbing the vegetables to a pulp through the colander. Cool, skim, season, and return to the fire. Heat, stir in the corn starch, wet up with water, and pour into the tureen. Add the milk boiling hot. Stir well, and serve.

Scotch Broth. — See under heading of *Soups and Broths.*

Stewed Prunes. — Buy box prunes, as they are of better quality than the open sort. Soak for an hour in cold water, put in a porcelain lined saucepan and add a little sugar. Let them stew an hour or more slowly, or until they are soft. These are very good in smallpox, measles, scarlet fever, and the like, not only as food, but as medicine also.

To make Gruel. — Time, 10 minutes. 1 tablespoonful patent groats, 2 tablespoonfuls cold water, 1 pint boiling water. Mix groats with cold water till smooth ; then pour boiling water on them, stirring all the time. Then set over fire in clean saucepan, and boil for 10 minutes. Sweeten to taste and serve.

Wine Posset. — In a pint of milk boil 2 or 3 slices of bread. When soft remove it from the fire, add a little grated nutmeg and a teaspoonful of sugar ; then pour into it slowly ½ pint of sweet wine and serve it with toasted bread.

Wine Whey. — 1 pint sweet milk, boil and pour sherry wine until it curdles ; then strain and use the whey.

"MY FAVORITE RECEIPT."

A COLLECTION OF 3,000 VALUABLE COOKING RECEIPTS.

This unique Cook Book has been compiled from the contributions received from our lady patrons in response to the request that they would send us one or more of their "favorite receipts" for publication. These contributions have come from every State in the Union, and from Europe, Asia, Africa, Australia, etc. Each receipt has attached the name and address of its contributor. Every department of cookery is considered, and methods are given for making the innumerable dishes in every conceivable practicable way. It will be found most remarkable for the large amount and wide scope of the information it contains. Being a compilation of formulas all thoroughly tested and vouched for by thorough housekeepers, "My Favorite Receipt" will be found to be the most essentially practical and valuable cook book yet published.

"My Favorite Receipt" is handsomely printed and bound, and will be sent to any address on receipt of price, fifty cents, in money or postage stamps.

ADDRESS: **ROYAL BAKING POWDER CO.**

106 Wall St., New-York, U. S. A.

Candies.

GRANULATED sugar is preferable. Candy should not be stirred while boiling. Cream tartar should not be added until syrup begins to boil. Butter should be put in when candy is almost done. Flavors are more delicate when not boiled in candy, but added afterward.

Butter Scotch. — 2 cups sugar, 2 tablespoonfuls water, piece butter size of an egg. Boil without stirring until it hardens on a spoon. Pour out on buttered plates to cool.

Cream Candy. — 1 pound white sugar, 3 tablespoonfuls vinegar, 1 teaspoonful Royal Extract Lemon, 1 teaspoonful cream tartar. Add little water to moisten sugar, boil until brittle. Put in extract, then turn quickly out on buttered plates. When cool, pull until white, and cut in squares.

Cream Walnuts. — 2 cups sugar, two-thirds cup water. Boil without stirring until it will spin a thread; flavor with Royal Extract Vanilla. Set off into dish with little cold water in; stir briskly until white and creamy. Have walnuts shelled; make cream into small round cakes with your fingers; press half a walnut on either side, and drop into sifted granulated sugar. For cream dates, take fresh dates, remove stones, and fill center of dates with this same cream. Drop into sugar.

Candied Horehound. — Boil horehound in water until juice is all extracted. Take your sugar and boil up to a feather; then add the horehound juice to the syrup; boil up till again the same height; stir with a spoon against the sides of the sugar-pan. When it begins to grow thick, pour out in a paper case dusted with fine sugar and cut in squares. The horehound may be dried and then put in the sugar finely powdered and sifted.

Candied Popcorn. — Put into an iron kettle 1 tablespoonful butter, 3 tablespoonfuls water, 1 teacupful white pulverized sugar. Boil until ready to candy, then throw in 3 quarts of nicely popped corn. Stir briskly till candy is evenly distributed over corn. Take kettle from fire, stir until it is cooled a little and you have each grain separate and crystallized with sugar, taking care that corn does not burn. Nuts of any kind prepared in same way.

Cocoanut Cream Candy. — 1 cocoanut, 1½ pounds granulated sugar. Put sugar and milk of cocoanut together, heat slowly until sugar is melted; then boil 5 minutes; add cocoanut (finely grated), boil 10 minutes longer, stir constantly to keep from burning. Pour on buttered plates, cut in squares. Will take about two days to harden. Use prepared cocoanut when other cannot be had.

Hickory Nut Candy. — 1 cup hickory nuts (meats), 2 cups sugar, half cup water. Boil sugar and water, without stirring, until thick enough to spin a thread; flavor with Royal Extract Lemon or Vanilla. Set off into cold water; stir quickly until white; then stir in nuts; turn into flat tin; when cold cut into small squares.

Chocolate Caramels. — 2 cups molasses, 1 cup brown sugar, 1 cup cream or milk, half pound chocolate, piece of butter size of an egg. Beat all together; boil until thickens in water; turn into large flat tins, well buttered. When nearly cold, cut into small squares.

Honey Candy. — 1 pint of white sugar, water enough to dissolve it, and 4 tablespoonfuls of honey. Boil until it becomes brittle on being dropped into cold water. Pull when cooling.

Ice Cream Candy. — 3 cups of sugar, crushed or cut loaf, a little less than ½ cup vinegar, ½ cups of cold water, piece of butter size of a walnut, flavor with Extract Royal Vanilla. Boil until it hardens, then pull until white.

Molasses Candy. — 3 cups yellow coffee sugar, 1 cup molasses, 1 cup water, half teaspoonful cream tartar, butter size of a walnut. Follow directions for cream candy.

Marmalades.

ORANGE MARMALADE. — Select best Florida or Seville oranges. Cut them in two, take out all the pulp and juice into a basin, pick out the skins and seed. Boil the rinds in hard water till tender, change the water 2 or 3 times while boiling. Then pound in a Wedgewood mortar, add to it the juice and pulp, then put all in preserving pan with double its weight of loaf sugar, and set over a slow fire. Boil ½ hour or more, put into pots, cover tight with brandy paper.

Transparent Marmalade. — Cut very pale Seville or Florida oranges into quarters; take out pulp, put in basin and pick out seeds and take off the peel. Put the peels in a little salt water and let stand over night; then boil them in a good quantity till tender. Cut into very thin slices and put them into the pulp. To each pound marmalade put 1¼ lbs. white powdered sugar, and boil for 20 minutes. If not clear and transparent in that time boil for few minutes longer. Keep stirring gently all the time, taking care not to break the slices. When cold put into jelly or sweetmeat glasses, tie down tightly with brandy paper, and over that a wet bladder.

THE ROYAL BAKING POWDER IS ABSOLUTELY PURE.

"ROYAL"

The Only Chemically Pure Baking or Yeast Powder Known.

The tests made by the Government chemists have shown that the Royal is the only baking powder made that contains neither alum, or lime, and is absolutely pure. Many of the powders prominently advertised as pure and wholesome contain alum, lime, phosphates, etc., and are unsafe for use in human food. These substances are used to make a cheap article, without any regard to the deleterious effect they may have upon the health of the consumer.

The superior quality of the Royal Baking Powder arises from the fact that only articles of the most wholesome character are employed in its manufacture, and that these articles are used only when chemically pure. The process of refining cream of tartar, by which all traces of lime are removed from it, is patented and controlled by the Royal Baking Powder Company. All the cream of tartar employed in other baking powders is refined in the old fashioned way, by which from five to ten per cent. of lime is inevitably left in it. Lime is therefore unavoidably one of their constituents.

Because of the supposed impossibility of removing the lime from cream of tartar when refined under the old processes, the Pharmacopœias have classed as "pure" cream of tartar that was not more than six per cent. impure. It is by the use of this definition (which is not now correct) that some chemists certify as pure those baking powders that actually contain this substance to a large extent.

REPORTS OF GOVERNMENT CHEMISTS.

It is a scientific fact that Royal Baking Powder is absolutely pure. I will go still further and state that, because of the facilities that company have for obtaining perfectly pure cream of tartar, and for other reasons dependent upon the constituents used in its manufacture, the proper proportions of the same, and the method of its preparation, the Royal Baking Powder is undoubtedly the purest and most reliable baking powder offered to the public.

HENRY A. MOTT, M. D., Ph. D.
Late U. S. Government Chemist.

I have examined the cream of tartar manufactured for and used by the Royal Baking Powder Company in the manufacture of their baking powder, and find it to be perfectly pure, and free from lime in any form. All chemical tests to which I have submitted it have proved the Royal Baking Powder perfectly healthful, of uniform, excellent quality, and free from any deleterious substance.

WM. McMURTRIE, E. M., Ph. D.
Chemist in Chief U. S. Dept. of Agriculture,
WASHINGTON, D. C.

I have tested a package of Royal Baking Powder, which I purchased in the open market, and find it composed of pure and wholesome ingredients. It is a cream of tartar powder of a high degree of merit, and does not contain either alum or phosphates, or other injurious substances.

E. G. LOVE, Ph. D.
Chem. for U. S. Gov't. Late Analyst N. Y. State B'd of Health.

BAKING POWDER TRICKS.

Many spurious baking powders are introduced by disreputable tricks. Peddlers travel from house to house, and try to prove by tests that their baking powder is as good as the Royal. The samples of their own goods carried for testing are specially prepared, by the addition of the white of an egg, gum, flour, or some other substance, to show some peculiar action, or by chemicals to destroy the odor of their gases when given off in testing. All first-class baking powders, when heated or mixed with water, will give off gases that are perceptible to the sense of smell.

These pretended tests are dishonest tricks. Their object is to destroy the baking powder found in the kitchen, to weaken the faith of the housekeeper in it, and to introduce an impure and often dangerous article in its place.

All who attempt to tamper with our food should be turned from the door, and their samples thrown away.

The Royal Baking Powder has been in use for a quarter of a century. Its absolute purity and wholesomeness are guaranteed by the impartial tests of the Government chemists, as well as by all Boards of Health. Careful housekeepers who desire pure and perfect food, and who have a regard for the health of their families, will use no other.

DANGER FROM ALUM AND PRIZE BAKING POWDERS.

The public is cautioned against buying baking powders by weight or bulk. All such powders are made from alum.

All baking powders sold with a prize or gift are to be avoided, as they are from 30 to 60 per cent. alum.

Alum baking powders are classed as poisonous by the most eminent physicians and chemists. They cost but three cents a pound to make, and, being sold at from 20 to 40 cents, are also a commercial fraud. They cause indigestion, heartburn, headache, dyspepsia, and diseases of the liver and kidneys. They may be known by the lower price at which they are sold, or by the prize that accompanies them, and by the bitter taste they impart to the bread or biscuit.

ROYAL IN ALL WAYS SUPERIOR.

I have made analyses of a number of samples of the Royal Baking Powder, purchased by myself from the dealers in Washington. I find it to be absolutely pure, containing no lime, no alum, or any injurious article whatever. The ingredients are only those proper for a baking powder of the highest degree of excellence as to wholesomeness and strength. Its entire freedom from lime and alumina, which are found in all baking powders made from commercial cream of tartar, from phosphates, or with alum, is an evidence of the remarkable perfection to which this most admirable baking preparation has been brought in respect to the purity of its ingredients, and renders it much superior to any other I have examined, or whose composition has been made known.

E. T. FRISTOE.
Prof. Chemistry Columbian University, and National Medical College,
WASHINGTON, D. C.

DO NOT USE
CREAM TARTAR AND SODA.

When these articles are adulterated, or servants are not particular to use the proper proportions of each, they will produce unwholesome cake and biscuit, with a disagreeable alkaline taste, full of yellow specks or reddish-yellow streaks. *Prof. Chandler, President of the Board of Health of the City of New-York*, states in his report, that upon investigation he found nearly all the Cream of Tartar sold by grocers was adulterated from 80 to 90 per cent. with white clay (Terra Alba), Alum, or other hurtful substances. These ingredients are very dangerous to health ; they impoverish the blood, produce Dyspepsia, serious Kidney complaints, and destroy the enamel of the teeth. Many housekeepers are of the impression that Baking Powder is a chemical compound dangerous to use ; this is true of the cheap kinds, which are mixed with the same ingredients used to adulterate Cream of Tartar.

Prof. Chandler, *in his report to the Board of Health*, strongly recommends the use of a well-known baking powder (like the Royal) in all kinds of baking, as being more convenient, economical, and much better than the old-fashioned methods. It is absolutely pure ; made from pure *Grape Cream Tartar*, and free from injurious substances of every kind. It is manufactured with the greatest of care, and in such exact proportions that it is impossible for a servant to fail with it.

The housekeeper should bear in mind that an absolutely pure powder like the Royal cannot be bought at the same price as the adulterated kinds. While the price of this powder is so low as to bring it within the reach of all, yet there are storekeepers who urge cheaper kinds, because the profits to them are larger. *The genuine Royal is sold only in securely labeled tin cans.* Baking Powder loose or in paper packages loses its strength and wastes. Refuse to buy it in that shape.

REMEMBER THIS.

In all your old receipts where cream tartar and soda or saleratus are called for, you can substitute Royal Baking Powder and get better results. The usual proportions in the old way are :

2 teaspoonfuls Cream Tartar,

1 teaspoonful Soda or Saleratus;

Instead of which

USE 2 TEASPOONFULS OF ROYAL BAKING POWDER.

and mix it with the flour while dry. This powder is so pure and perfectly combined, that one-third less of it will do better work than cream tartar and soda.

COMPARATIVE WORTH of BAKING POWDERS.

ROYAL (Absolutely Pure)..
GRANT'S (Alum Powder) *..
RUMFORD'S, when fresh...
HANFORD'S, when fresh....
REDHEAD'S ....
CHARM (Alum Powder)*....
AMAZON (Alum Powder) *...
DAVIS', and **DAVIS' O. K.** New York. (Alum Powders.)*
CLEVELAND'S.........
PIONEER (San Francisco)...
CZAR...... ....
DR. PRICE'S. ....
SNOW FLAKE (Groff's) .....
LEWIS'...... ....
PEARL (Andrews & Co.)......
HECKER'S............
GILLET'S ....
ANDREWS & CO. "Regal"* Milwaukee. (Contains Alum).
RUMFORD'S, when not fresh

REPORTS OF GOVERNMENT CHEMISTS
As to Purity and Wholesomeness of the Royal Baking Powder.

"I have tested a package of Royal Baking Powder, which I purchased in the open market, and find it composed of pure and wholesome ingredients. It is a cream of tartar powder of a high degree of merit, and does not contain either alum or phosphates, or other injurious substances.   E. G. LOVE, Ph.D.

"It is a scientific fact that the Royal Baking Powder is absolutely pure. The Royal Baking Powder is undoubtedly the purest and most reliable baking powder offered to the public.   H. A. MOTT, Ph. D.

"The Royal Baking Powder is purest in quality and highest in strength of any baking powder of which I have knowledge.   WM. MCMURTRIE, Ph.D.

The Royal Baking Powder received the highest award over all competitors at the Vienna World's Exposition, 1873; at the Centennial, Philadelphia, 1876; at the American Institute, New York, and at State Fairs throughout the country.

No other article of human food has ever received such high, emphatic, and universal endorsement from eminent chemists, physicians, scientists and Boards of Health all over the world.

NOTE.—The above DIAGRAM illustrates the comparative worth of various Baking Powders, as shown by Chemical Analysis and experiments made by Prof. Schedler. A pound can of each powder was taken, the total leavening power or volume in each can calculated, the result being as indicated. This practical test for worth by Prof. Schedler only proves what every observant consumer of the Royal Baking Powder knows by practical experience, that, while it costs a few cents per pound more than ordinary kinds, it is far more economical, besides affording the advantage of better work. A single trial of the Royal Baking Powder will convince any fair minded person of these facts.

* While the diagram shows some of the alum powders to be of a comparatively high degree of strength, it is not to be taken as indicating that they have any value. All alum powders, no matter how high their strength, are to be avoided as dangerous.